Life on a Permanent Wave

Hair-raising Stories
from a Shipboard Stylist

By Richard Wood

with Tracey Hawthorne

First published in 2014

Copyright © text Tracey Hawthorne and Richard Wood, 2014

Copyright © photographs Richard Wood, 2014

In some cases, names have been changed, to protect the privacy of the people concerned and ensure the authors don't have their butts sued off.

All rights reserved. No part of this publication may be reproduced, stored in a retrieval system, or transmitted, in any form or by any means, without the prior written permission of the copyright holders.

A Life on the Ocean Wave,

A home on the rolling deep,

Where the scattered waters rave

And the winds their revels keep.

From 'A life on the Ocean Wave'

by Epes Sargent and Henry Russel, c1840

Contents

Prologue

1. Embarkation

2. The Salon

3. The Crew

4. The Cabins

5. The Penthouses

6. The Theatre, Casino, Gym and Spa

7. Public Rooms: Restaurants, Bars and Lounges

8. Below Decks

9. The Bridge

10. The Infirmary

11. The Outside Decks

12. Disembarkation

A potted history of the *QE2*

Glossary of South African terms

About the authors

Prologue

In the Steiner hair salon on the *Queen Elizabeth 2* – the *QE2*, the most famous ocean liner in the world – there were two banks of ten hairdryers each, and although we were always very busy, it was rare that all twenty of the dryers were in use at the same time. The two nearest my station were used only when absolutely necessary.

One particularly frantic day I discovered one of these dryers to be occupied – under it sat a little Japanese lady, neat as a pin in her kimono, her shoes slipped off and her feet tucked up under her. When the buzzer went after forty minutes, the salon was in full swing. 'Whose lady is this?' I called, making myself heard above the noise of the other hairdryers and general chit-chat, but no-one responded.

At times like these, when we were all busy with clients, sometimes attending to three or four people simultaneously, we'd help each other out by quickly and quietly resetting the timer on the hairdryer. The reason for this was simple: many of our clients were very demanding Americans, who expected, the second their drying was finished, to have a stylist hop to and immediately finish working with their hair. So switching the thing off and asking them to wait for ten minutes until you had some time to attend to them wasn't an option.

So I reset the timer for another thirty minutes.

When the buzzer went off for the second time, the little Japanese lady was beginning to look distinctly red in the face. 'Whose lady is this?' I called again. Some of the other stylists looked up, harassed, from their stations, but nobody claimed her, so, giving her a cheery smile, I reset the dryer for a third time.

Half an hour later, the buzzer went off again. By now the lady was beginning to turn an interesting shade of puce, so I called, 'Hey, guys! Whose lady is this? She's beginning to cook!'

This time I got everyone's attention, including that of the receptionist. Opening the appointment book, she ran her finger down the day's column of bookings and matched the relevant one to the stylist. She gave me a withering look. 'You idiot,' she said. 'She's yours!'

Escorting this uncomplaining Japanese woman out from under the dryer, where she'd been steadily desiccating for almost two hours, I thanked my lucky stars that she wasn't American – if she had been, I'd still be trying to get the boot out of my arse.

1. Embarkation

When a ship leaves land, it becomes a floating village. And on a cruise liner like the *Queen Elizabeth 2*, known as 'the city at sea', which was my home-from-home for twelve years, the hair salon is the wildly beating heart of that community. At some stage during a cruise, most of the passengers will drop by, for a quick trim or a full-on styling, and often just to exchange shipboard gossip.

When I started my career on cruise liners back in the 1980s, there was an additional attraction in the hair salon: women. Of the 1 050 general crew on board the *QE2*, only fifteen were female. One of these was the captain's secretary; seven were the women who worked in the various boutiques and shops; and seven were employed as hairdressers. (There were also two professional nurses and several female casino staff, but they were considered to be 'outside' of general crew.)

The salon was a honey pot: the staff were young (21 to 30), open to fun and the bizarre, and mainly attractive – the biggest uniform size was 8, and if you couldn't fit into a size

8, you were considered unemployable. Aside from the seven women, there were five men, four of them gay.

And the salon was an attraction not only for the thousand-odd male staff, it was every bit as much a focus of attention for many of the 1 800 passengers the ship carried at full capacity. What was it about walking up that gangway that put a glint in the passengers' eyes? The throb of the nine multi-cylinder diesel engines, each the size of a double-decker bus? The thrum of the two propulsion motors? Or was it simply the concept of being apart from the usual, adrift in a self-contained little world, that caused passengers to behave in ways they would never have considered back in their 'normal' lives? People who work in the land-based hospitality trade report the same phenomenon: when guests enter a hotel room, they leave their reserve at the door.

And the dearth of men didn't stop passengers getting their jollies, either. Some of the crew took full advantage of this, and staff who were dyed-in-the-wool heterosexuals on land weren't beyond becoming boy-toys at sea. An onboard masseur, Justin, for instance, who was inordinately proud of his (admittedly very large) penis, would whip out this impressive organ for anyone to see, sometimes even before being asked. Word quickly spread through the decks that Justin wasn't hobbled with many inhibitions, and it wasn't unusual to spot so-called straight men entering the massage-therapy room with a hundred-dollar bill tucked into their towels. They'd emerge half an hour later, the money gone and a look of happy satisfaction on their faces.

Indeed, as I learnt during my years at sea, gender, age and state of health were no barrier at all when it came to the sexual energy generated by being aboard. Once, an 82-year-old man came into the salon after having spent an ill-advised day lying on a deckchair in the sun. His face was cracked and peeling, his lips bloody. 'I've got some cream that will help with that,' I said to him, kindly, and he rewarded my concern with a repellent leer. 'I'll take it on one condition,' he creaked: 'that you deliver it personally to my cabin after 8 this evening – and apply it.' And he was nothing compared to the octogenarian stroke victim whose hair I had the misfortune to have to trim: although unable to speak and confined to a wheelchair, this horny old codger always managed to use his one good hand to make a grab at my crotch while I, standing as far as humanly possible from the wheelchair, tried to do my job.

It wasn't what I'd expected when I first decided that I wanted to become a ship's hairdresser. But I was clueless about quite a bit back then: at the tender age of 21, when I qualified as a hairdresser in Port Elizabeth, I had the distinction of having won the South African Apprentice Hairdressing Championships, an achievement that was printed in the local newspapers, along with a picture of me. With this, I thought I could go anywhere – and my first stop was going to be Steiner, one of only two companies worldwide that held hairdressing concessions on cruise liners at the time.

I'd been clued in to the glamorous life of being a shipboard hairdresser by my friend, mentor and fellow hairdresser, a Briton called Leigh, who had done a three-week 'incentive' cruise with the Cunard Line – owner and operator of the *QE2* – and decided that a life on the ocean wave was for her. She was too young at the time to apply for a permanent job (men had to be 21 and women 25 before they were considered for fulltime shipboard employment) and had opted to come to South Africa and work as a hairdresser for the four years before she would be eligible. What I learnt from her about her three weeks on board the *QE2* was enough to make me certain that *that* was what I wanted to do too.

Full of confidence and enthusiasm, I moved to Cape Town and found employment in a salon there. In the meantime, I wrote a letter to the Steiner headquarters in London, offering them my invaluable services as a shipboard hairdresser. Their response? A chilly silence.

I was disappointed but not discouraged. What I didn't realise was that there were only about thirty fulltime positions for shipboard hairdressers at any one time on all of the big cruise liners combined, so the competition was extremely stiff.

Then another ship hove to on my horizon and strengthened my resolve. This one came courtesy of a Cape Town customer of mine, a travel agent, an old queen who would have done practically anything to get into my knickers. While I never succumbed to his questionable charms, an invitation I did accept from him was to a gathering of travel agents at which several lucky-draw prizes of ocean-going cruises were up for grabs. And I won one.

Two weeks cruising on the *Astor* and I knew that this was the only life for me. When I got back on land, I wrote to Safmarine, the South African company that owned the *Astor*, and offered *them* my not-to-be-missed hairdressing services. Their response? They sent my application letter on to Steiner.

This time, however, I had more luck, and Steiner responded to say that I should go in for an interview 'the next time I was in London'. They may as well have said 'the next time I was on the moon': an air ticket to London then cost R3 000, a sum that was so far out of my reach that even thinking about it hurt my wallet.

Then fate intervened in a typically South African way: my house was burgled. My insurance paid out for what had been stolen, and the cheque they sent me was in the sum of exactly R3 000. I took this as a sign. I was 23 years old and my dream finally seemed in reach.

I sold up the few possessions I had left and flew to London. I made an appointment with Steiner and turned up for my interview, confident that this was no more than a formality. I dressed for the occasion as I imagined any slightly eccentric, will-try-anything-once young hairdresser might do, in jeans and a denim jacket (very outré at the time); I didn't shave, thinking that a bit of a morning shadow would lend me some boho credibility. As a hairdresser, I felt it part of my job to challenge the butch male South African stereotype, and my interview outfit showed this, I thought, to excellent effect.

Bear in mind that this was the 1980s – the decade, some say, that fashion forgot. Women either power-dressed in business suits with shoulder pads large enough to land aircraft on, or followed Madonna's 'Material Girl/Virgin' example and put their bras on last. Men either emulated Boy George and piled on the mascara, or did a 'Miami Vice', with expensive suit jackets over pastel T-shirts; Hawaiian shirts in eye-blindingly bad taste were also all the rage. Hair was big, eye shadow was blue, and shell suits were stylish.

Again, my ignorance let me down: London hairdressers, and especially those who were employed by Steiner, were (and are) a quintessentially professional bunch. Gay or straight, they all *appear* straight; they wear suits and ties to work, and their personal grooming is always immaculate.

My interviewer took one look at me and said, 'Thanks but no thanks.' And then completely floored me by telling me that Steiner 'didn't employ South Africans'. Perhaps my dropped jaw and the look of panic in my eyes stirred pity in her, because she then told me that if I were able to find a position in a Steiner salon in London, and work there for a year, my application for shipboard employment would be considered.

No problem! I was young, I had time on my side, and anyway, working in London would be great experience. Fired anew with enthusiasm, I immediately began the task of getting myself a work permit.

Easier said than done: for various reasons, I didn't qualify for one.

I continued harassing the Steiner people nonetheless, trying to find a loophole through which I could crawl onto a cruise liner. And what I discovered was that I could indeed secure a position as a trainee in a land-based Steiner salon – but that while I was training, I wouldn't be paid.

Even that didn't put me off. The money I'd taken with me to London was fast running out, but I'd find a way. I submitted my application papers to the Steiner people – who declined, for reasons I never discovered, to sign them.

I was reaching the end of my tether. I'd been in London for five months, and for most of that time I'd been running all over the city to various bureaucratic departments, travelling long, confusing, exhausting distances by Tube and bus and train, standing in queues and filling out forms. This was also at the height of the apartheid era, when South Africans were very much *not* flavour of the month, and I began despairing.

Still, I never stopped pestering Steiner, and phoned them regularly to enquire about the possibilities of employment with them. Finally, one of the many people I spoke to sent me for a 'trade test', a very tough few hours at a Steiner salon in a massive, busy shopping centre, where I was required to venture out into the throngs of shoppers and randomly find a volunteer who would agree to allow me to style their hair under the critical eye of a senior stylist. Not surprisingly, there weren't many English shoppers who, confronted by a clearly rather desperate young South African, agreed to let me bugger around with their crowning glory. Finally, however, a game woman with longish hair dyed in black and white stripes that made her look like nothing so much as a skunk, gave me the okay, and I spent an extremely stressed half-hour putting her hair into an 'up' style.

When it was done, I stood back and surveyed the result with some pride. I was, after all, the winner of the South African Apprentice Hairdressing Championships, and I knew what was what when it came to 'dos.

'You done?' asked the supervising stylist, giving my lovely up-style an unimpressed look. I nodded. He whipped a pencil out of his pocket, stuck it into the top of the 'do and jiggled it around, much like he was stirring a cup of coffee. A few strands came loose. 'Rubbish,' he snapped. 'This would never stand up to a hurricane.'

In spite of this, I passed the trade test, and was told to fill out an employment application form and attach a recent photograph of myself, which Steiner said they would 'put on file until something came up'. I knew they were just trying to get me off their backs but what did I have to lose?

I didn't have a recent photograph of myself, so I attached to the form the newspaper clipping that showed me, full of youthful pride and optimism, when I'd won the Apprentice Hairdressing Championships. And two days later I received a letter from Steiner, telling me to get my affairs in order because they'd booked me on the *QE2* for a three-week trial run. The ship was leaving from Southampton for New York in six days.

Six days! In that time, I had to organise not only a US visa, but also kit myself out with four pairs of black trousers and eight white shirts (I cringed when I read that, realising how profoundly I'd misunderstood the dress code when I'd gone for my first interview), and a full complement of hairdressing equipment – and all of mine was back in South Africa. And I didn't have a cent to my name.

A London friend came to my rescue with a loan of a very generous thousand pounds. (His kindness taught me a lesson I've never forgotten, and I'm always willing to lend money to friends in need.) With that cash injection and the golden promise of a crew berth on the *QE2*, I managed the superhuman task of organising everything I had to.

The great day dawned, and some South African expats – many of them political exiles, some having left the motherland to avoid the mandatory two-year military conscription for all white male school-leavers, and others journalists who were on the lam from the law for having written unacceptably truthful reports about the state of the country at the time – drove me to Southampton to meet the ship.

There, my ignorance hobbled me once again: faced with the confusion of the docks in Southampton, I didn't have a clue how to get on the boat. Becoming more frantic as time ticked by – I'd been instructed to present myself for embarkation at 0900 on the dot – I stopped and asked dozens of people, none of whom could help me. When I finally found my way onto the ship it was noon – I had got on board three hours late for embarkation, an ignominious start.

That was my first embarkation but over the course of the next twelve years I'd do countless more. I'd also be on hand to wave departing passengers off the ship and welcome new ones coming on board. After I was appointed assistant manager of the hair salon, I was expected, along with other senior-ranking staff, to form a guard of honour for our embarking and disembarking guests. One of these senior staff members was a Czechoslovakian called Marc, an assistant restaurant manager whose uniform resembled an officer's, dress whites with epaulettes. And if that weren't droolicious enough, Marc also had the kind of good looks that meant he was often mistaken for a movie star.

Marc, whose own bedroom preferences ran to groups rather than one-on-one experiences, taught me quite a bit about the pulsating sexual energy on board ship. There we would stand, proud and young and gorgeous, shoulder to shoulder, smiling and shaking hands and nodding with exemplary courtesy to the arriving passengers. And under his breath, Marc would be pointing out the tasty ones to me. 'That's one for you…' he would murmur, raising his eyebrows surreptitiously at some gorgeous young thing (often coming up the gangway arm-in-arm with his wife), '… and that's one for me,' and, turning with a dazzling smile to whichever unknowing bit of fluff had reached our point in the guard of honour, would say with unctuous good manners, 'Good morning, Mrs So-and-so. It's a pleasure to have you on board. Enjoy your cruise.'

Marc also taught me the modus operandi for sexual conquests on the four-night, five-day North Atlantic crossings. It was important, he pointed out, to have 'fun without the fallout'. To do this, he said (with wisdom, I assumed, acquired by trial and error), it was important never to strike on the first night – if you did, you might get saddled with a lust-struck passenger who would hound you for the rest of the cruise.

So, the first night on board, I learnt, was dedicated to a bit of light stalking: we'd find out where the pretty passengers were accommodated and hang around just enough to be noticed. On the second night, on the understanding that absence makes the heart grow fonder (or, as Marc had it, 'makes the frond grow harder'), we'd observe strict confinement to our cabins. On the third night, we'd mix and mingle in the various public lounges and bars (always keeping our eye on our stalkees) but maintain an alluring aloofness. And on the fourth and last night, it was full steam ahead.

On the fifth and last day of the cruise, many passengers disembarked with satisfied and knowing smiles. And there were a lot of secret little waves given by certain members of the crew, too.

Not that working life on the *QE2* was all just hot sex on tap – not by any stretch of the imagination. Another of the jobs of the greeting crew was to deliver to each cabin a bouquet of flowers or basket of fruit to welcome embarking guests. This was no small task – sometimes there were over 700 of the things to get in place before the passengers started arriving, and it wasn't always possible to do it before they did. Crew would scurry around madly, carrying towering bouquets and cornucopias of fresh produce, desperate to get them delivered to the cabins ahead of time. Arriving at a cabin door to deliver the welcoming gift after the passengers were already ensconced was an exercise in hand-wringing and butt-kissing that everyone tried to avoid, although it wasn't always possible.

Worse, though, was when friends or relatives sent a gift of flowers or something similar to be delivered when the ship was already en route, because then we'd have to abandon all pretensions of being staff members of the world's most famous cruise liner and act as if we were trainee waiters at our local Spur. It was de rigueur to sing 'Happy birthday' if the gift arrived on a birthday; and if it was an anniversary or some other celebration, we'd have to sing 'Congratulations and celebrations'. Those were never my finest hours.

Still, we got our own back in a small way. We'd get the pre-cruise passenger manifest and scan it for celebrities and other VIPs. Forewarned, they say, is forearmed: and we were. When Names came on board, we'd be careful to treat them with studied disdain. They were on *our* territory, and we made sure, in subtle ways, that they knew it.

2. The Salon

That first cruise was also my first trans-Atlantic crossing, on what is known as a 'shakedown' cruise. These shakedowns happen after the boat has completed one of its world tours and the permanent staff take time off, leaving a skeleton crew behind, along with a full complement of trainees.

All fulltime shipboard staff fell into one of three 'leave parties' who did alternating stints of two-months-on, one-month-off; all staff, that is, except the hairdressers, who worked 12-hour days, seven days a week, month in, month out. And for this back-breaking schedule, I was told I'd be earning £35. Wow, I thought, £35 a day! It was an unimaginable fortune for a completely broke young South African – and unimaginable is precisely what it turned out to be, because my wages were, in fact, £35 a *week*. (To put this into perspective, I'd spent £15 on a hairdryer before boarding.)

One thing that quickly became very clear to me was how vital punctuality was on board ship – throwing into stark relief the heinous sin I'd committed before I'd even put foot on board, by being three hours late for embarkation. Hairdressers had to present themselves at the salon 15 minutes before the 8am opening time: one minute late meant we lost our lunch hour; any more than a minute late and all free time was immediately rescinded. Our working hours were so long and arduous that every free moment was preciously guarded, so it was absolutely essential that we get to work on time.

Which wouldn't have been a problem had the ship's clocks been in anything like agreement. There were clocks all over the ship; all of them were controlled from the bridge, and no two clocks ever told the same time. One of the problems was that most of the clocks were simply old and didn't keep time accurately any more; another was that because we were continuously crossing time zones, the clocks were continually being changed an hour this way or that – and the person doing the changing wasn't particularly bothered to make sure the change was accurate to the minute. So more than once I skidded into the salon with, I thought, time to spare, only to be told that I'd lost precious 'off' time. 'But the clock outside my cabin said 7.40am!' I would wail; and Jen, a trainee manageress who was determined to use this trial cruise to make her mark, would point at the salon clock and say, 'I don't care what that clock said, *this* clock says you're late.'

It was a measure of how valued time off was that when Steiner offered its employees incentives in the way of products or cash, productivity didn't measurably increase. When, however, off-time was offered instead, you've never seen a salon of hairstylists work so damned hard.

Time became particularly confusing when the ship crossed the dateline and gained or lost a day, depending on whether it was travelling west or east, meaning that there were sometimes, for instance, two consecutive Tuesday 30 Mays. Trying to get *which* Tuesday 30 May – the first or the second – was the day of their appointment into some passengers' heads required much patience. And that's not even to go into when we lost a day – when, for instance, there was no Friday 15 June, and the week's calendar skipped straight from Thursday to Saturday. 'What do you mean, there's no Friday?' a passenger trying to book an appointment would ask indignantly, as if we were personally responsible for subtracting an entire day from their lives.

Jen the trainee manageress was, it was generally agreed, a bit of a nightmare. Fortunately for me, she took a shine to me. This had less to do with my scintillating personality than it did with my natural inclination to be a bit piraat, and also because, after my compulsory two years in the South African Defence Force, I'd learnt a thing or two about saying 'how high?' when a superior asked me to jump. So I didn't mess around – if Jen instructed me to do something, I did it immediately.

By contrast, a lot of the English guys on board regarded the trial cruise as just that – a cruise. Perhaps they weren't as hungry as I was; for me, this was the beginning of my career; for them, it was just a three-week adventure before they moved on to more serious things. So when Jen gave them an instruction, they'd get around to doing it – eventually; usually after a smoke break somewhere out of sight of Jen's beady eye.

My willingness to allow Jen full rein with her own ambitions helped me with mine: at the end of the three-week trial period I was promoted to assistant manager of the salon. This was a significant step up and, although it (disappointingly) didn't come with a concomitant increase in salary, it did confer on me full deck privileges, which meant that I was to be a 'front man' for the salon. Whereas most of the other thousand-odd crew members were specifically trained to be invisible, disappearing below decks whenever they weren't actually on duty, in my new position I was to be a full part of the passengers' day-to-day lives at all times, joining them for cocktail parties, eating dinner with them and playing host at the various functions held on board. And for this, I was always to be dressed in either a suit or a full tux.

It was a very heady experience for someone who not many months before had regarded denim togs as the last word in sartorial splendour. Two years after I'd first set my sights on becoming a shipboard hairdresser on a luxurious ocean-going liner, I'd finally made it.

§

Over time I became accustomed to the annual patterns of the *QE2*. During the relatively milder northern summer, the ship crossed the North Atlantic. The package offered to tourists at the time was the cruise from Southampton to New York (or vice versa), and a return flight by that other trans-

Atlantic legend, the supersonic Concorde. This attracted a disparate group of people across a wide age group, and anybody from 18 to 80 might be on the ship for these crossings. They were particularly popular with Americans.

For some passengers, this northern crossing was a matter of necessity, not luxury. One I remember in particular was Mrs McNabb (whose signature hairstyle was a Flapper-Girl 'do, and who trusted me with the job of turning her naturally grey but heavily highlighted Afro-style mop into a wavy confection of pin curls). She had survived an aeroplane accident in her youth and as a result had sworn off air travel for life.

The world cruises, which ran during the northern winter when the North Atlantic was notoriously rough and inhospitable, attracted the older set. Between December and March the ship would ply the world's seven seas, offering a range of routes to clients under a variety of clever monikers: 'Follow the Sun', say, or 'Spirit of the Great Explorers'. Then, the *QE2* might, for instance, leave from New York and travel south, through the Panama Canal and across the Pacific to Japan, India, the Seychelles, the east African coast and South Africa, then across the south Atlantic to Rio de Janeiro, before returning to New York.

The world cruises were a popular way of getting the older members of rich families out of the northern cold for a while

– instead of sending them to Florida, their families would stow them safely on the *QE2* for a few months.

One of these was a Mrs Gibbons, of a famous consumer-goods manufacturing empire. A divorcee in her late 60s, with one daughter and one grandson, she was under no illusion as to why she'd been shipped off on the *QE2*: 'They [her family] want to forget about me,' she would complain. She wasn't wrong: although she would write almost daily to her grandson, the apple of her eye, she never got a reply; and in the four months she would spend aboard each year, she never once received a phonecall or a visit. She wasn't my favourite person but I couldn't help feeling sorry for her.

This old stick had very light-blonde hair, and I remember her distress when she returned once from a game safari through the reserves of Kenya: her hair had turned brick-red. Deprived of her salon appointments for the four days of the safari, she hadn't had her usual daily shampoo-and-set, and the ironstone-and-laterite African 'murrum' soil, turned to dust by the heat and kicked up by the wheels of the safari vehicles, had impregnated her hair, turning her into an almost-unrecognisable redhead. So thoroughly had this natural treatment permeated her locks that two weeks later, despite daily salon visits, she was still vaguely titian.

Because the salon was situated on 1 Deck, G Stairway, it was pretty central, and passengers were forever coming into the salon reception and asking for directions to other parts of the ship. We didn't mind doubling as the ship's informal information centre, but I was always amused when people expressed surprise to find a hair salon on board. 'Wow, a hair salon!' they would say, as if it were the last possible thing they might have imagined finding on a gigantic luxury cruise liner.

But the truth was that practically anything that could have been found in a small, very efficient little city could also be found on the *QE2*, from plumbers, electricians, engineers and carpenters to doctors, nurses, dentists and physiotherapists. The staff complement included waiters, public room and cabin stewards; there was a full laundry staffed and run by bona-fide Chinese laundrymen; there were dancers and singers, printers, photographers, computer technicians, cruise salesmen, florists and seamstresses. There were formal dining rooms, elegant bars and lounges, boutiques, a European-style spa, a casino, a grand ballroom, a cinema, a computer centre, indoor and outdoor swimming pools, a shuffleboard court, a tennis court, a golf driving range and putting green with an in-residence pro golfer, a synagogue, one of the largest libraries at sea with over 6 000 books and a trained librarian… you name it, the ship had it.

And all the people who serviced this floating city ate, lived, worked and slept on board for as long as the *QE2* was cruising. Some of the passengers could hardly believe that such a large staff complement existed side-by-side with them, most of them quietly and invisibly going about the job of making their clients' cruise experiences as enjoyable as possible.

One woman asked one of our hairdressers, in disbelief, 'So do all you people sleep on board?'

It was one of those 'snappy answers to stupid questions' moments (and we got a lot of them), and this stylist stepped quickly up to the plate. Keeping a perfectly straight face, he answered, 'No, madam. There's another ship that follows us, and every night at midnight we're lifted off the *QE2* by helicopter and taken to the staff ship to sleep.'

The next morning, a very irritated purser came to remonstrate with us. 'I had a passenger in my office first thing this morning, complaining that she hadn't been able to sleep a wink last night – because the noise of the "staff helicopter" taking you guys back to the "staff ship" had kept her awake!'

One of the less pleasant aspects of being in management in the salon was all the hand-holding we had to do for the greenies – the trainees, often straight out of school, who'd spent a few months with Steiner in London before being sent down to Southampton to join the *QE2*. On these first outings, the chaff would be separated from the wheat: not only would potential employees have to do their job up to standard, but that standard would have to be what was expected on the *QE2*.

Many of these kids were hardly out of their teens and had to be coaxed every step of the way: woken up (sometimes forcibly) each morning, succoured through the almost-inevitable bouts of seasickness, patted on the back when they cried from homesickness, quietly rescued when they made a terrible hash of someone's hair, dragged down to the infirmary when they took too many drugs or drank too much... If at times I felt like a pimp in the salon, there were also times when I felt like a kindergarten teacher. Some of them, poor little sausages, just couldn't cut it: it wasn't unheard-of for a greenie to buckle under the pressure and beg to be put ashore – the shortest period of employment on my watch was a greenie who lasted three days before crying 'uncle'.

One of these greenies – not a hairdresser, but a public room steward – was a young German kid whose dream, he told anyone who would listen, had always been to work on the *QE2*. But for reasons I don't know, it must have all just proved too much for him. Pretty soon he was showing signs of depression and, tragically, he finally hanged himself in his cabin.

And sometimes it was necessary to be a detective, too. When someone didn't turn up for work and wasn't to be found in their cabin, we'd have to track them down. This involved finding out who they'd been partying with the previous night; then whittling this down to who they were last seen with before everyone went to bed; then working out what department that person was in, so that the correct cabin could be found; then, finally, finding the cabin and banging on the door loud enough to wake up the usually shagged-out couple who lay within.

There were also indelibly memorable characters and one of these was Aiden, who just happened to be the son of a preacher. A wild boy, he had the letters 'LOVE' tattooed on the knuckles of one of his hands (without the serial-killer Harry Powell-style 'HATE' on the other, I'm happy to report) and several earrings in each ear. A land-based style director for Steiner, he objected fiercely to having to remove this jewellery during his annual four-week 'guest' cruise on the *QE2* – in Aiden's mind, he was a star, someone for whom the usual rules didn't apply. Although gay, he was madly popular with all the staff, and could often be found late at night in the crew bar, a bottle of poppers jammed jauntily into a nostril, surrounded by adoring bimbettes, belting out 'the Steiner song' ('Nothing could be finer/ than to wake up with a Steiner…').

Aiden had a secret weapon, one that I discovered some years later, when, for my 29th birthday, he insisted on squiring me around London's gay club scene. We started off at his very chi-chi flat in Kensington, where he doled out the evening's chemical entertainment: one beer, one joint and one ecstasy tablet each. (Aiden instructed me sternly that I was not to have anything else after this, and clearly he'd hit on the right mix after studious years of trial and error, because it worked a treat.) Then we piled into a taxi and headed for Soho, where we trawled the clubs – including Heaven, which was and still is a long-standing London tradition – until they closed.

One of the things I remember about those ecstasy-fuelled clubbing days was that many of the night-spots had had the cold-water taps in their toilets soldered closed. Like any street drug, ecstasy (or MDMA) wasn't without its risks, and users were repeatedly warned against drinking alcohol if they'd taken an ecstasy pill. Part of the reason for this was that MDMA was known to cause dehydration, a potentially dangerous condition that can be exacerbated by alcohol.

Add to that the fact that ecstasy made you want to dance for hours – and so, usually, sweat buckets – and the need for water became very clear. London clubs, quickly realising that they were losing alcohol revenue because their super-smiley hippie-hoppy-happy patrons weren't drinking anything but good old H_2O, soldered shut their cold-water taps and began selling bottled water – at a pound a pop, serious money in those days.

As sensible as drinking water may sound, however, there's just no telling what people zoned off their heads on tablets might do: Leah Betts, an 18-year-old UK schoolgirl, became the poster-child for the anti-ecstasy campaign when she died after taking one pill – not as a direct result of the MDMA on her body, but after drinking about seven litres of water in just ninety minutes to counteract dehydration.

Back at Aiden's flat, my host rolled down a giant sleeper couch, and we tore off our clothes – which is when Aiden revealed a penis that would have put a donkey to shame. I was very, very impressed, and all I could do was point, and say, in awe, 'Aiden!'

Aiden stood there in the altogether, very proud and humble, saying, 'I know! I know!'

Aiden now owns a salon in the UK and, twenty years on, is still every bit as wild.

Another memorable trio from the crew were the Jones brothers, Greg, Tony and Ray: the sons of a London chambermaid. Greg was a wine steward, and Tony and Ray were waiters. They worked on board for five years and we became close friends. Greg's claim to fame was being able to skin up a joint single-handed and undetected in his jacket pocket – in a storm. (His signature saying was, 'When you've had enough, it's time for more!')

Once or twice I went to stay with them in their council flat in London, where I had my eyes well and truly opened to what living in 'council housing' really means. The family lived in a small, run-down apartment in one of the infamous tower blocks that were both held responsible for and held up as examples of the 'urban blight' that plagued London during the Thatcher years. It was little wonder the brothers so enjoyed being at sea.

There were, of course, unforgettable characters among the passengers too. The late Barbara 'Bobo' Rockefeller was a frequent cruiser. Then in her 70s, her claim to fame was having married into the famous American family – a union that earned her a *Time* magazine cover and a portrait by Salvadore Dali. Born Jievute Paulekiute to Lithuanian immigrants, she'd married Boston socialite Richard Sears Jnr and become a minor Hollywood film star during the Second World War. Her second marriage, to millionaire Winthrop Rockefeller, was shortlived but culminated in what was a record divorce settlement for the time: $5,5 million in the 1950s.

Known in her heyday as 'delightful and difficult', she was just difficult by the time I met her on the *QE2*, when she was dividing her time between homes in New York and Paris – she would embark in New York and disembark in Cherbourg, then travel to Paris for the season's fashion shows.

Although she largely shunned the press, she was nonetheless known for giving pithy soundbites. If she felt she were being overcharged for some item, she would snap, 'Who do you think I am, a Rockefeller?'

Barbara's hairstylist while she was in New York was celebrity coiffeur Mr Kenneth – but she would only let him cut her hair, not colour it. When she wasn't a passenger on the ship, she would telex me ahead of time and I would meet her in New York, ready with a ship's pass for her, and she would come on board for her appointment. She would tell people, grandly, 'Mr Kenneth of New York cuts my hair; Richard of the *QE2* colours it.'

This was a woman who insisted, 'I intend to be Mrs Rockefeller until I die.' And, indeed, when she died at the age of 91 in 2008, she was still Mrs Rockefeller.

Mrs Rockefeller may have had a point about our ability with colour, even if I say so myself. We would stock up on tints and dyes in Southampton before we left on the four-month world cruise. The base shades were numbered from 1 to 10, with 1 being the darkest and 10 the lightest; and then there were a range of other tints, from red to gold and copper, that we used to obtain a specific end result. The number 7 base shade was the most popular, so inevitably that's the one we ran out of first. We would then mix numbers 6 and 8 to get a tint as close to number 7 as possible. But by four months in, we were often getting very low on those stocks too, and towards the end of the cruise it wasn't unthinkable to find a stylist-turned-alchemist furiously mixing numbers 1 and 9 and creatively adding a variety of other tints to come up with a suitable colour for a client.

Despite this unconventional approach, our clients were almost always delighted with the end result, and we were even sometimes asked to provide the 'recipe' for a client's particular hair colour – which, of course, was often impossible to do. 'Please,' a happy customer would beg: 'my colourist at home has never got just this tint, and I love it!'

And we would just look suitably solemn and whitter on about Steiner patents and trade secrets.

Another female client who found fame by dint of having married a famous man was Peggy Johnson, the second wife of iconic businessman and chairman of the Chrysler Corporation Lee Iacocca. Iacocca's beloved first wife, Mary McCleary, had died in 1983 from complications from diabetes, after 27 years as Mrs Iacocca. Lee (whom Peggy called 'Lido') met Peggy, a flight attendant 26 years his junior, in the offices of the Statue of Liberty Commission, where she was volunteering. At the time, Lee was the chairman of the fundraising campaign to restore Ellis Island and the Statue of Liberty for their 1986 centennial celebrations.

The *QE2* was moored in New York's Hudson River for the 4 July unveiling of the statue, renovated at a cost of $62 million, with Peggy, Lee and hundreds of other dignitaries on board, including Bill Clinton, who was then the Governor of Arkansas (he would become the 42nd president of the United States seven years later, in 1993). It was the culmination of a unique charter for the ship – Iacocca had rented it to ferry 800 Chrysler dealers and their spouses from Southampton. The party had, in fact, started in Paris, and from there had followed 'the historical trail of the Statue of

Liberty', which had been a gift from the French to the people of the United States.

The second Mrs Iacocca sticks in my mind for the simple reason that the events organiser forgot to make a salon appointment for her ahead of the gala dinner on the evening of 3 July. With the salon already booked well over capacity, we had no choice but to make space for this Name, who wanted the works – hair, makeup, manicure and pedicure.

A short eight months later, Peggy was relegated from the ranks of the rich and famous when the marriage collapsed. Peggy afterwards blamed the failure of the union on Lee's continued devotion to his beloved late Mary, whose possessions, she said, were preserved in the master bedroom of their mansion while she, Peggy, slept in a former maid's quarters.

It was around that time that New York was also known as the 'murder capital' of the USA – the city's homicide rate reached an all-time high not long afterwards. This inherent danger became very clear when the ship attempted a ferry-shuttle service for crew who wanted to go ashore overnight, and within five minutes of the first shuttle's docking, four of the people who'd gone ashore had been mugged and in two cases stabbed. The shuttle service was immediately discontinued.

One other unique charter I remember, although I don't recall the details, was when some lunatic millionaire chartered the ship for 24 hours for his daughter's bat mitzvah – her *13th birthday party*! Fifty guests rattled about on the ship, where everything, including all the restaurants, salons and shops, had to stay open round the clock. Nothing, of course, was paid for by the revellers, and the tab for both the 24-hour charter and all consumables was picked up by the doting daddy.

A lavishly obnoxious passenger was Mrs Ringley, who couldn't open her mouth without a complaint issuing from it. She would have a regular anthracite rinse at the salon – a procedure that, using one teaspoon of the active ingredient, creates the much-loved-among-the-elderly mauve rinse, but which amount the never-satisfied Mrs Ringley demanded should be upped to a cup. The result was that her hair came out a violent purple, much like Dame Edna Everage's.

This whingeing woman came into the salon one day, and our receptionist, Mandy, a lass with a very broad Yorkshire accent, greeted her by name. "Ello, Mrs Ringley,' she said. "Ow can I 'elp ye?'

Mrs Ringley scowled at the cheerful young woman. 'How do you know my name?' she demanded stridently.

Mandy, who was well aware of Mrs Ringley's reputation for querulousness, replied, 'Well, Mrs Ringley, you're the only lady aboard wi' fookin' purple 'air!'

Mrs Ringley, hard of hearing and unable to unravel the accent, could do nothing but glare suspiciously at the girl.

This same Yorkshire lass, a strapping young woman who looked like she came from good farming stock, once 'helped' a dithery old passenger from the beauty salon across to the hair salon in a ferociously efficient manner. The old dear, a Miss Seal, was quite infirm, and often held up the works in the salon by taking ages to wobble cautiously from one room to the other, which drove us crazy because we were always very busy and other passengers hated to be kept waiting for their appointments.

On this day, Miss Seal was making her slow, trembling way to the salon after having had her nails done, when Mandy decided she just couldn't take it any more. She marched over, pushed her large, capable hands into Miss Seal's bird-like armpits, and, lifting her bodily off the floor so her little old feet flapped helplessly in mid-air, she raced her into the salon, saying as she did so, 'Ayup, Zola!' – a reference to Zola Budd, the South African barefoot runner who was in the news at the time. (One of the skills we learnt in the salon was how to keep a straight face.)

Miss Seal, who travelled with two companions and two personal maids, loved the attention she got in the salon even if we couldn't really do much for her. She was such a quavering old stick of a thing that the minute the manicurist had put the final coat of varnish on her nails, one of Miss Seal's trembling fits would smudge them. And she had so little hair that it took only two minutes and only two rollers to prepare it for the dryer.

We had another client who, like Miss Seal, was all but devoid of hair and more than a little nutty. Mrs Hunter had so little hair left – just a few wisps in the front – that she always wore a wig. Nonetheless, one of the first things she did when she stepped on board was visit the salon – to buy all our brushes and combs. And I mean *all*: no matter how many we had in stock, Mrs Hunter would take them all away with her.

Mrs Hunter's husband, Jack, died unexpectedly at the very beginning of one of the world cruises, and it was a devastating blow for the dear old lady. For the rest of the cruise, she could be seen following various elderly men about the deck, calling after them, 'Jack! Jack! Jack!'

§

Retail sales were an important part of the Steiner business: because the ship claimed 40% of our takings from styling but only 10% of those from retail, we were encouraged to sell as much product as possible.

At the time, Steiner had three 'magic' goodies in its vast beauty bag: 'California Sun Glow', a translucent red-tinted powder that came in a gorgeous little pot with its own sable-hair brush; an anti-frizz hair serum; and a heat-activated anti-wrinkle cream called Micro Dermazone which delivered observable if temporary results.

So when some old dear came into the salon, looking pale and wrinkly and with hair awry, the first thing we'd do, as we conducted the consultation, was dab a few dots of the Micro Dermazone under her eyes and elsewhere on her face where the lines and creases were particularly obvious.

That done, we'd get started on her hair, and when it came to blowdrying, would be careful to aim the jet of heat at the pretreated bits on her face. Once her hair was finished, with any frizziness banished thanks to liberal use of the serum, we'd sweep some California Sun Glow over her eyelids, cheekbones and chin to give her a bit of colour. And voilá! Pale, frizzy, wrinkly old lady suddenly looked like Joan Collins: smoothly coiffed, with a silky and glowing complexion.

Another favourite retail item in the salon was a range of diamanté-studded hair accessories. Quickly a competitiveness evolved among the stylists – whoever could cram the most of these little hairpins into the 'do of a customer would win. By the time I left the ship, the record stood at 24.

Our customers bought these products by the truckload – so much so, in fact, that Steiner won the Queen's Award for Export in 1991! Some of the Steiner higher-ups were invited to Buckingham Palace to accept the award, and we staff were each presented with a pin to commemorate it, which we wore on our uniforms.

Steiner had other alliances with the Royal Family, which were proudly displayed in the salon: in 1947 Herman Steiner (son of Henry, the founder of the company), was granted a Royal Warrant as hairdresser to Queen Mary, and in the 1970s he got a second Royal Warrant, as cosmetician to the Queen Mother.

§

One way of making sure that the salon – and every other department on board – stuck strictly to the five-star service the *QE2* demanded was passengers being invited (and sometimes bribed with offers of various 'prizes') to fill in ratings and comments sheets once they'd completed their cruise. Everyone was aware of these, and of the effects they could have – a bad passenger rating or negative comment could earn a department a black mark or even get someone fired.

It was rare that a staff member conducted themselves so unacceptably that they was put off the ship, and it took Justin – he of the outsized member – to behave so badly that not only was he put ashore, but he was kicked off in the very next port of call, an exceptionally rare occurrence.

Usually, should a staff member be fired during a cruise, they were removed from active service until the ship returned to Southampton, where their services were officially terminated.

Most staff members, when faced with an irritating or unreasonably demanding passenger, stuck strictly to their training and remained polite and calm, no matter how heated the discussion might get. Not Justin: criticised for his massage technique by a demanding client, he simply turned around and told the passenger to fuck off.

He was astonished when he was summarily 'bridged' – summoned to the bridge for an official dressing down and dismissal – and even more so when he wasn't even allowed to mooch about on board until the ship got back to headquarters in Southampton: rather than have him anywhere around the passengers, the unusual decision was taken to put Justin ashore in New York and fly him back to the UK.

As hard as we tried to do our jobs up to scratch, there were, of course, unavoidable logistical glitches, both in the salon and elsewhere on the ship.

One of the most difficult for Steiner was when, for reasons never communicated to us, the water supply unexpectedly ran out – which happened with embarrassing frequency. Then, we'd have to escort our clients with hair in various stages of transformation to the pool deck, seat them on a chair, and rinse them off with buckets from the swimming pool. It was pretty insalubrious treatment for people paying a fortune for a silver-service cruise.

And then there were, before the 1986 refit of the ship, the hair-shampoo sinks, which were bolted to the floor. Which wouldn't have been a problem had the chairs in which our unwitting customers sat for what should have been a relaxing hair wash and gentle head massage also been fixed to the floor. But they weren't, so every time the ship rolled, the chairs moved – but our customers' necks, jammed in the hollow in the sinks, didn't. I can't count the times I waited for the ominous *click* sound that would signify some poor old dear's neck snapping.

Also, the Steiner airconditioning ducts must have been connected in some way to the galleys – because at precisely 3pm every afternoon, the rank stink of onions and garlic would flood the salon. As pleasant as these smells might be in a working kitchen, they clashed horribly with the floral scents of our products.

But most passengers were understanding about these things, and Steiner seldom got poor ratings or negative comments from clients. I'm not going to be falsely modest here: in the twelve years I worked aboard for Steiner, I became something of a 'celebrity hairstylist' myself. My appointment book was always chockablock but I valued my regular clients and always made a special effort to fit them in.

This lovely letter, written on *QE2* stationery, was from a passenger I'd attended to after the salon had officially closed, because she'd returned to the ship late from a shore excursion.

Dear Richard

I cannot thank you enough for doing a perfect job on my hair again. I received so many compliments and it is so manageable. In fact, I was up on the bridge in a 50mph gale and it combed out nicely five minutes later!

I hope to see you on the trip to Norway in July. I will ask for you the minute I step on board.

It took me vividly back to the day I'd done my 'trade test' as a young hopeful in London, and the Steiner supervisor had stirred the up-style I'd created with his pencil and declared it unfit to stand up in a hurricane – suddenly, it all made perfect sense!

Another time, I received under my cabin door a letter written by the hotel manager to a Dr and Mrs Tanner – who had specifically requested my services on their next tour. 'Further to my letter of yesterday,' it read, 'I am pleased to advise you that I have spoken to the managing director of Steiner and he agrees to have Richard on board during the next World Cruise – providing, of course, that Richard wishes to be here. I am therefore confident that you will indeed have the services of Richard next year.'

As gratifying as these compliments were, it got to a point, at one stage, that I was simply overstretched – I was working the usual twelve-hour days, plus putting in overtime, which included, in some cases, going to a client's cabin to do her hair, and still passengers were opting to wait a few days for my services rather than accept an earlier appointment with one of the other stylists. Something had to be done, and Steiner took what they thought was a canny business decision to solve this problem: they gave me my own price list, with everything on it marked up by 20%. The idea was that customers who were prepared to pay a premium to be serviced by me could do so; the others, it was thought, would be happier to settle for the relatively less expensive services of my colleagues.

It backfired – Steiner hadn't reckoned with that peculiar form of snobbery that demands 'only the best', meaning 'only the most expensive'. So even those skinflint passengers who were lifting *QE2*-branded salt-and-pepper sets from the dinner tables and smuggling *QE2*-monogrammed towels off in their luggage, and who under normal circumstances wouldn't deign to tip a waiter, suddenly simply *had* to have me do their hair.

Within a few weeks, my waiting list was longer than ever, and the 'Elite Richard Wood Price List' was quietly abandoned.

A possible reason for my superior hairstyling skills (if such they were) came clear some years later, in 1990, when, after a few weeks of much-needed home leave, I prepared to fly from Cape Town back to London to rejoin the ship. There was something going on at the airport that resulted in long queues and delayed our departure; it was only once we were in the air that I learnt that then-South African President FW De Klerk was on board. I didn't catch so much as a glimpse of him – he was, of course, in First Class, while I was stuck with the rest of the plebs in steerage – but there were plenty of dark-suited security men with gadgets in their ears in evidence.

We had to wait, again, at Heathrow, while the Prez was escorted safely off the plane first. This made me late for a meeting at Steiner, which annoyed me, but I suppose world leaders are allowed to inconvenience us little people as much as they feel is necessary for their own comfort and safety.

(As an aside, this reminds me of the visit to South Africa of US President Bill Clinton in March 1998, when for two days the city of Cape Town practically ground to a halt as a result of the attendant security – which included, if reports at the time were to be believed, the welding shut of manhole covers on roads that would be taken by the President and his cavalcade on their journey into the city centre.

Capetonians were not impressed when they had to sit in endless queues of traffic to get to and from their places of work, be rerouted along complicated detours, miss meetings, and in some cases abandon any hope of getting to work at all.)

The following day I made my way to Southampton to join the *QE2*, which was just completing a charter to Spain, Portugal and Morocco sponsored by the Texas chapter of the Young Presidents' Organisation (YPO), a group of businessmen who had realised extreme wealth and/or success before they turned 45. Having already had my journey twice delayed by De Klerk's entourage, I was irritated to find a similar hullabaloo happening in Southampton: helicopters hovered, roadblocks abounded and several routes into the harbour were cordoned off. It took me a good 45 minutes to board, and by the time I did, I was really pissed off.

'What the hell's going on here?' I asked a fellow crew member.

'You should know,' he replied. 'It's your President!'

Coincidentally, De Klerk had been making for the very same destination I had: he'd been invited to give a speech to the gathered members and guests of the YPO on board the *QE2* to finish off the cruise.

There were, among the YPO faculty on board, a certain George W Bush, then a managing general partner of the Texas Rangers baseball team whose father was President of the USA. There were also several South African members.

Now, it's no secret that many of South Africa's most successful businessmen and businesswoman are Jewish: this famously entrepreneurial group of people began arriving in the country in the 1800s and quickly made their mark as commercial pioneers in industries as disparate as mohair production, sealing, whaling and fishing, ostrich-farming and diamond-mining.

The wealth they generated enabled them to live well, and, among elder-generation South African Jews, gave rise to the initially derogatory term 'kugel' to describe a woman who had become overly materialistic and excessively groomed. Nowadays, 'kugel' is used in a lighter way to describe a (usually) youngish Johannesburg Jewish wife whose sole focus is on her appearance, and who spends her time gymming, shopping, lunching with the ladies and, of course, in the salon.

So, apparently, there were a number of kugels on board the *QE2* for this charter, the wives and girlfriends of the South African YPO members. And they were extremely exacting about what they wanted from the Steiner stylists.

'Now we know why you're so good at your job!' an exhausted onboard hairdresser said to me as I finally made my way to the salon through the throngs of people on board. 'Those South African women! Cheesh! They were the most difficult clients we've ever had!'

Still, as hard as our job sometimes was, with its endless client demands and long hours and occasional pretty hectic work conditions, those customers who took the time to express their gratitude made it worth it.

There's always one, though – and in this case it was a passenger who wrote a lengthy complaint about her hairstyle 'not lasting', because when she went out onto the open deck 'soot from the funnel landed in my hair'. We stylists were able to perform many small miracles in the course of our seaboard duties but controlling flying smuts wasn't one of them.

§

One vividly difficult time in the salon had nothing to do with styling, products or customers. In 1986 the ship underwent a huge overhaul that changed its propulsion system from steam to diesel-electric – and, in the salon, our accounting system was changed, at the same time, from manual to computerised.

The age-old system of 'dockets', on which all details were written, along with their prices, had served the salon very well for years. Tallying up credit-card slips and cash at the end of the day, to ensure they matched the information recorded on the dockets, was never my favourite task, but even my very rudimentary maths skills were up to the job.

With the 1986 overhaul, the ship got its own computer system, which included a mainframe that linked all money-taking areas. When customers came on board, they handed over their credit card, which was swiped, and they were given a Cunard card for use throughout the voyage. This Cunard card, which could be used anywhere in the ship, for any product or service, would be linked by computer to the customer's account, which, at the end of the voyage, would be debited with the full amount.

This made things much easier for the passengers and simplified Cunard's accounting system – but it was a nightmare in the salon. With takings, sometimes, of up to $10 000 in a day, trying to balance the Cunard card entries with the ordinary credit-card ones (customers could still use their credit cards independently if they chose), plus cash, was a nightmare. In the beginning, while we were getting used to the system, it wasn't unusual for me to spend an entire night in the salon trying to track down an elusive few dollars – Cunard insisted that all books be balanced daily to the very last cent. I recall once leaving the salon at 4am, having spent eight hours trying to find $45 that couldn't be accounted for. California Sun Glow cost $45 a pot, and I roundly cursed whatever stylist had sold that product that day.

3. The crew

'You're not gay, are you?'

They weren't words to warm my heart, but they were the first ones the person who would be my cabin-mate for three weeks, Peter, said to me. And his evident homophobia wasn't the worst thing about him; his utter and complete disregard for personal hygiene was. This dirty creature didn't shower *once* during our three-week stint at sea, and he treated his wardrobe with as little respect: he chucked his suitcase into a corner, and over the next two weeks picked clean clothes off the top; in the third week, when he ran out of clean clothes, he simply rummaged around at the bottom of the pile to find the cleanest dirty clothes, and wore those.

Peter's shower-shirking was evident to me, because it was my unhappy lot to live in close quarters with him – but apparently it wasn't that obvious to the guy who would become his best mate on board that cruise, Steven, a young man who ran one of the shops. Steven, who came by our cabin in the third week of the cruise (by which time Peter was very, *very* dirty) to wake up his pal, chose a novel and stomach-turning way to rouse him from his heavy slumber.

Peter was lying on the top bunk, his feet dangling over the edge, and Steven, thinking to playfully wake him up, did this by sucking his big toe!

Another hellaceous cabin mate I had was Stewie, a relentless seeker after casual sex. Regardless of the fact that I occupied the top bunk in our shared quarters, he would bring a different person back to the cabin every night and bonk them brainless – then, when all the excitement was over, he would reach up and bash the underside of my bunk and crow, 'Did you hear that, Japie? *Did you hear that?!*' ('Japie' was one of my nicknames – I was for many years the only South African on board.)

Stewie's other quirk was his total inability to wake up early in the morning and even the last-ditch desperate measure of setting *three* alarm clocks didn't work – he just slept through all of them. Finally, he employed our 'glory-hole' steward (the person whose thankless task it was to clean the staff accommodation) to wake him up – by literally coming in and hitting him. It was disconcerting to watch the glory-hole slip into the cabin, coathanger in hand, and bliksem Stewie with all his strength – but it was even more so when Stewie finally opened his eyes and, lifting the blanket, drawled, 'Okay, I'm awake now. I've got five minutes – want to slip in?'

Every bit as dissolute was Justin, the onboard masseur with the very large penis. He took to dropping by my cabin during his off times to 'practise his orgasm faces' on me. Contorting his features in imaginary ecstasy, he would ask me, 'How's this one? And this?' Sometimes he'd try out a long, slow journey to his sexual peak, by which stage I'd be on the floor, tears rolling down my face. At other times his pretend-climax would be short, sharp and rather violent, and I'd be pulling faces of my own, in a combination of amusement and disgust.

Staff cabin inspections took place once a week, while the inhabitants of the cabins were at work. Sometimes just a head of department would do the inspection; at others, the department head was accompanied by an officer. These cabin inspections, conducted mainly for reasons of safety and hygiene, were pretty serious: if your cabin failed inspection, you were liable for a written warning; three written warnings and you were put off the ship.

When just the head of department – in Steiner's case, that was sometimes me – did the inspections, nobody bothered much. In fact, I'd use the hour allotted to cabin inspection to get a bit of a lie-in: I'd sleep until ten minutes before the hour was up, then stick my head into each cabin, pronounce it fine, and that was it: inspection done.

Doing cabin inspections with the officers was a lengthier process – but not always because they were particularly looking for slip-ups. The officers would take these opportunities to closely examine what was, in effect, the private lives of their crew: their photographs of their friends and loved ones, the books they were reading, the clothes they wore on off-days.

Still, sometimes the inspections did throw up potential dangers, such as a curling iron left on and closed in a drawer or a tap not switched off. And sometimes they just revealed embarrassments, such as when an officer and I let ourselves into the cabin of Ricky, then head of the gym, and found him not only lying sprawled in his bunk when he was supposed to be at work, but energetically engaged in a solo sex act that should have remained private.

§

Sometimes we wished we *did* have a staff ship following us. Most of the crew were accommodated in pretty basic two- and some four-berth cabins, with showers and toilets at the end of each alleyway. These cabins were located forward and aft on Decks 3, 4, 5, 6 and 7. If you were unlucky enough to be allocated an aft cabin, sleep was often difficult because of the noise and vibration of the two propulsion motors, each weighing over 400 tons (the largest marine motors ever built) and each capable of producing 44MW of power and driving the ship forward at a top speed of about 32 knots. In those cabins, it was necessary to literally Prestik your alarm clock to your bedside table, in order to prevent its being rattled off by the vibrations. The forward cabins weren't much better – it was these that took the full brunt of the ship's nose plunging repeatedly in and out of waves at high speed, and staff who were allocated these soon became accustomed to being routinely flung out of bed.

Even if I weren't close enough to the propellers to be kept awake, there were times when I'd go up onto the deck rather than try to sleep through a storm – down below things could feel quite hairy and I had no wish to end up as a bit player in another *Poseidon Adventure*. I was always very aware of the gigantic power of the ocean, and notwithstanding the *QE2*'s enormous size, it still ground through the waves in bad weather. Sometimes I'd lie there, listening to the groaning and creaking of the metal that made up the ship's superstructure, and wonder how thick it actually was – thick enough not to cave in?

As it happens – no.

The year was 1995 and the then-Steiner manager, Patsy, and I were having dinner together when we got a 'blue slip' warning us of bad weather ahead.

'Fuck,' I said, and Patsy grimaced in agreement.

Bad weather warnings were a right royal pain in the arse. At the slightest hint of turbulence ahead (the bridge received regular telexed forecasts from the Met Office), 'all seamanlike precautions' had to be taken. For us in the salon, this meant battening down – which translated into several hours of fussy, boring, arduous work, and often for nothing. Not only did all the furniture have to be corralled and cupboards locked, but the fragile and friable contents of no fewer than eighteen professionally window-dressed displays had to be taken down and safely stowed. If this happened after hours, as it did on this occasion, it was even worse – our staff had gone off, and Patsy and I had to do it all ourselves. And the next morning, before we opened for business for the day, the entire rigmarole had to be done again, in reverse, so that our first customers were presented with a salon in tiptop shape.

So we were very tempted to ignore this particular warning. Because Cunard would be financially responsible for breakages in the salon that occurred if weather warnings *weren't* given, we got dozens of false alarms, and there was no reason to believe this wasn't another one. It was terribly tedious – I can't count the number of times we stowed the salon for no reason at all. But good sense prevailed, and Patsy and I abandoned our dinner half-eaten and spent a couple of hours making sure that the salon was secure.

That done, we went to one of the bars, the Yacht Club, for a final drink. There, I got an inkling that this weather warning might be genuine: the ship's 2IC came past and when we invited him to join us, he declined. 'I'm going to wedge my life jacket and try and get some sleep,' he said. 'This is no weather to be out in.' Crew quickly learnt, when the seas were rough, to wedge their life jackets under the mattress on the open side of their bunk, creating a slope in the mattress that effectively held the sleeper in the bunk when conditions got rough enough to toss stuff around.

Our captain at the time was Commodore John Burton-Hall, a highly respected sea dog with a terrifyingly gung-ho attitude to sailing. His battle cry on entering heavy seas was, 'Remember: three hands! Two for yourself and one for the ship!' (meaning you had to hold on for dear life). His trust in the *QE2*'s abilities to handle high seas was frankly frightening, and his attitude of 'Bugger the Atlantic! Full steam ahead!' was entertaining when it wasn't scaring the pants off us. (And it would have made Sir Samuel Cunard, the original founder of the shipping line who died in 1878, turn in his grave: Samuel's exhortation was, 'Speed is nothing… safety is all that is required.')

Perhaps fortunately for us, we had a relief captain during this incident – Captain Ronald Warwick (whose father, incidentally, had also helmed the *QE2*), a cautious man who slowed the ship to a near-idling speed of about four knots to maintain steering into the mountainous seas, in preparation for what lay ahead. Even so, by the time Patsy and I had finished our drinks in the Yacht Club, I was having to brace myself not to be jolted out of my seat. This jarring was caused when the ship crested a wave and then crashed back down into the water, its gigantic propellers smashing down into the sea. For all its majestic size, the *QE2* was still just a boat on a vast, immensely powerful ocean.

Patsy and I said our goodnights and went to our respective cabins. There, tired by the long day, the fast, arduous work of battening down the salon, and the loopdop in the Yacht Club, I climbed into my bunk and fell asleep – but not before remembering the advice of the 2IC and wedging my life jacket.

When I woke up I was on the floor. Groggily, I looked at my watch: 4am. Barely conscious, I replaced my mattress, wedged the life jacket back, and climbed back in.

The morning dawned serene: I looked out my porthole and the sea was as smooth as glass. 'Those bastards!' I thought. 'Another battening-down for no good reason!' I hadn't slept well and felt irritable, so when I met Patsy for breakfast I was all set to moan my head off about the wasted effort we'd put in the night before. But there was something about her white-faced appearance that made me hold my tongue. 'What?' I asked.

'What?!' she said. 'Where were you, in a parallel universe? We hit a tidal wave last night!'

It was Hurricane Luis – a very rare, very large, very intense storm that formed part of a two-week tropical cyclone that caused extensive damage in the Caribbean with winds of up to 215kph, and left hundreds missing and tens of thousands homeless.

The damages to the *QE2*, too, were severe. The watch on the bridge told us later about their astonishing 'three swells' experience. The first was like riding the world's wildest rollercoaster, they said, but the ship plunged into it and came out fine; the second was bigger and greatly more frightening. But nothing prepared them for the third: a hundred-foot wave that broke onto the prow of the ship, sweeping objects (including the anchor) from the deck and punching a huge hole in the front. 'Out of the darkness came this great wall of water,' Captain Warwick later said, comparing it in size to the White Cliffs of Dover. 'I have never seen a wave as big as this in my whole life.' It was the impact of that wave that had knocked me out of bed.

I went below with Patsy to examine the damage. A vast web of wooden scaffolding was holding battens in place, masking a gigantic gash in the front of the ship.

Hurricane Luis went down as one of the biggest hurricanes in modern history. And I slept through it.

(This is perhaps particularly ironic as my father, Graham, was drowned in a boating accident when I was 4 years old: a keen deep-sea fisherman, he was miles from land one day when a freak wave capsized his boat. His body was recovered ten days later.)

Previous to Luis, Hurricane Gloria in September/October 1985 was the heaviest weather the *QE2* had sailed through. Gloria had wreaked havoc along the east coast of the United States, directly affecting New York and Long Island. Out in the Atlantic, the hurricane reached Force 10 in the early hours of 2 October, with, according to the ship's log, 'very rough seas and very heavy swell; ship rolling and pitching heavily; spray overall.'

There were, of course, other dangers on the high seas. One was whales. I was interested to read a newspaper report in 2001, after I'd left the ship, about the *QE2* colliding with a fifteen-ton, sixty-foot whale during a cruise from Spain to Portugal. Apparently it had sailed into Lisbon with the dead whale still pinned to its bow. The master of the ship, Captain Keith Stanley, who admitted that some of the passengers had been 'saddened' by the incident, told reporters with bizarre understatement, 'It's one of those things, like running over a cat.'

That wasn't my experience some years earlier, when, on a trans-Atlantic voyage, the ship suddenly began moving strangely. The passengers were probably not aware of it, but for those of us who'd become entirely accustomed to the normal pitch and roll of the vessel, and the feel of the propellers' vibrations under our feet, we knew something was amiss. There was an unusual jarring sensation as the ship moved through the water.

Lengthy investigation finally revealed a whale pinned against the ship's prow. Word quickly got out and soon passengers were crowding the front of the ship, trying to get a glimpse of the unfortunate creature. Many of them were extremely distressed, even after they'd been assured by the captain that the whale was quite likely either very ill or already dead by the time the ship collected it – whales are known, he told them, to evade ships. (I discovered subsequently that this isn't strictly true: whales are regularly hit by ships all over the world's oceans.)

We were already behind schedule and the captain decided to speed up the ship in the hope that this would shake off the corpse of the whale. Alas, it didn't work: the pitching and yawing became worse, and the passengers increasingly unsettled.

So, finally, the *QE2* did what it uniquely among cruise ships could do: it slowed, stopped, went into reverse and sailed backwards at high speed. (The *QE2* could sail backwards at 19 knots, which is faster than most cruise ships can sail forwards.) The whale carcass came free and quickly sank from sight, and the ship continued its voyage to New York.

§

Incidentally, Patsy's alleged headboard notches included blue-eyed UK actor Terence Stamp, who came on board not long after his stellar turn as a cross-dresser in the Australian surprise indie hit *The Adventures of Priscilla, Queen of the Desert*, which took overseas box offices by storm and won an Oscar for costume design. In it, Terence plays Ralph/Bernadette, a radical departure from his usual macho roles – but he brought to the part a masculine cynicism which was as characteristic as it was funny.

In the movie, Ralph/Bernadette and companions are being harassed by a yobbo called Frank, and Ralph/Bernadette tells him, 'Stop flexing your muscles, you big pile of budgie turd. I'm sure your mates will be much more impressed if you just go back to the pub and fuck a couple of pigs on the bar.'

Bob, one of the *Queen of the Desert* contingent, says, 'Bernadette, please!'

Frank is beside himself at this. '*Bernadette!*' he exclaims. 'Well, I'll be darned! The whole circus is in town!' Then he turns to Ralph/Bernadette and says, 'Well, I suppose you wanna fuck too, do you? Come on, *Bernadette*, come and fuck me. That's it. Come on. Come and fuck me. Come on.'

Ralph/Bernadette steps up and knees Frank really hard in the balls. 'There,' he/she says. 'Now you're fucked.'

Terence Stamp in the flesh isn't that far removed from his Ralph/Bernadette character; and, interestingly enough, Patsy herself bore more than a passing resemblance to *Priscilla*'s Bernadette. They were more than a match for each other.

While there was plenty of licentious behaviour on board between crew and passengers, passengers and passengers, and crew and crew, there were also genuine romances – not surprisingly, given that many of us spent most of our time on board. I had two long-lasting relationships, one with a bartender called Terry Brown which lasted a pretty tumultuous and entirely unrequited three years, and another with another Terry, Terry Doyle.

Terry Brown was miffed when I ended our relationship and took up with Terry Doyle, and he made no bones about this – despite the chaste nature of our union – remarking snidely one night in the Fo'c'sle Bar, 'What is it, just the name you like?'

It wasn't, but I should have left well enough alone. Instead, I began the rather silly habit of calling Terry Brown 'Mr Brown' and Terry Doyle 'Mr Doyle', so that the two could be differentiated in conversation. My relationship with the second Terry took a turn for the worst, however, one night when, in the heat of the moment, I mistakenly called him 'Mr Brown'. So I was sad but not entirely surprised when Mr Doyle went off with a dancer not long afterwards.

Another love affair I had was with a gorgeous young thing called Charlie. This one happened at a time when we'd been instructed that cruise staff wasn't 'allowed' to be gay – if we were, we'd do well to hide it.

Charlie got me with glo-sticks, those translucent plastic tubes that contain two chemicals in separate compartments which, when cracked, mix together and produce a bright green, yellow, orange or blue chemoluminescence. If you've got kids, you'll know about them; otherwise, you might have seen people wearing them around their necks or wrists, or just waving them about, at rock concerts or sports matches. We on the *QE2* were familiar with this phenomenon in nature, when bright-green 'milky seas' were sometimes created by groups of plankton.

After a wild night out onshore in Southampton once, Charlie took me back to his cabin and told me to wait in the bathroom until he said it was okay to come out. In my absence, he *broke open* (not just cracked) about 10 glosticks and, holding them with their open ends outwards, spun around the cabin, scattering the luminescence all over the roof, floor and walls. Then he switched off the lights and called me out. I opened the door onto a fairyland of neon stars. How could I have resisted?

Charlie – who was wildly popular with all the gay boys and many of the women, and was fairly enthusiastically pursued by several of them – started getting stalker-type anonymous letters pushed under his cabin door at one stage. 'I want to tie you up and go down on you,' read the first one, which we laughed about. The second was slightly more sinister: 'Think I'm joking?' it read. 'You are my fantasy man and I'm going to have you – whether you like it or not.' The third one, which isn't fit for publication, was alarmingly explicit and really rather terrifying.

The letters were typed, and Charlie (a fan of detective novels), examining the third one closely, realised that the 'e' was slightly out of kilter with the rest of the text. 'Hey, how many typewriters can there be on this ship?' he asked, excitedly, and immediately made it his business to track down the specific machine that had been used to produce the notes.

It took several weeks, but Charlie did finally find the machine: it was in the purser's office, in plain sight; but the purser's office was open all day and sometimes late into the night, with much coming and going, and anybody could have used the machine to type the letters.

Charlie, not a man to be swayed from a task once he'd set his mind to it, asked Liesel, the American Express rep on board, to keep an eye on the typewriter for him. She chose to accept this mission, and by the end of the week had narrowed the list of possible suspects down to ten people.

She gave this list to Charlie, who, flicking through the names, quickly fingered the suspect: Marvin, the night hotel officer, who was known to paw boys – and Charlie in particular – late at night in the public rooms once he'd had one or two too many.

Charlie had a quiet word with Marvin later that same day and, as far as I know, the letters – and the drunken harassment – stopped. I wish I knew what Charlie said to him, but it was a subject on which he wouldn't be drawn.

I had another relationship, with the entertainments manager 2IC, a man called Ray but whose nickname was 'Wrinkly' – because, at all of about 40, he was considered by the crew to be old! This relationship was frankly sexual in nature – I liked Ray, but more than that, I liked having sex with him. Fortunately for me, he was as keen, and we'd often pop into his cabin for a quickie in between our onerous daily duties. (Once, embarrassingly, we were having it off in his cabin while the ship was preparing to leave a port; unbeknown to us, we were clearly visible through the porthole to everyone standing on the dockside. That was one departure that couldn't happen quickly enough for me.)

At the same time, Jen the manageress was having a relationship with the entertainments manager, Rob. Jen and Rob often had lunchtime assignations in Rob's cabin – which happened to abut Ray's. Jen would return after her lunch break, click-clacking in on her stiletto heels, a Cheshire-cat grin on her face, and murmur to me as she went past, 'Smile if you got it at lunchtime.'

I was, of course, aware of the close proximity of Rob's cabin to Ray's, so one lunchtime, when Ray and I were getting it on in his cabin, I tried to keep the noise level down – apparently, however, without success. As I sauntered back into the salon after lunch, Jen gave me a wicked look and said, 'Smile! You got it at lunchtime!'

§

One staff member who came on board with the express objective of bagging for herself an officer was a glory-hole steward called Tonya. She was unusual in being a female staff member in what was then an exclusively male occupation – the fact that the officers' glory-hole steward's accommodation was a single cabin and therefore didn't have to be shared with another staff member was the sole reason she'd got the job.

The first we knew of this extraordinary creature was, one filthy night when a few of us were out on 3 Deck Aft, having a quick spliff while trying to keep our feet out of the water that sloshed across the deck with every wave, and wrapped up against the driving rain, she appeared in our midst, swathed from neck to ankle in a very expensive-looking fur coat. In spite of her lowly occupation – glory-holes were, basically, wannabe cabin stewards – she made no secret of the fact that she considered herself a cut above most of the staff, being answerable as she was to the officers.

The other women on board – the Steiner girls and boutique assistants – quickly closed ranks: they didn't want anything to do with Tonya, whose vivacity was tempered with a commonness that made everyone feel uncomfortable and whose frequently-stated aim of ending up as an officer's consort irritated most of us. Not only that, but she employed her coarse come-hitherness in a curiously scatter-shot way, with the result that several 'lesser' (in Tonya's eyes) men, including deck hands and engineers, responded to her flirtatiousness, only to be humiliated by her, often publicly.

Perhaps, as a result, she was just lonely, but I still felt uneasy when she decided to befriend me and conferred on me a questionable privilege: that of 'accompanying' her when she had her bubble baths. The only lockable bathroom (in that it had a genuine standalone bath, not a bath with a shower installed over it as in most of the shared ablutions) was next-door to my cabin, and Tonya had somehow procured for herself a key to this small room. The first time she knocked on my cabin door and asked me to 'keep her company' while she bathed, I was amazed to find, on going next-door some minutes later, Tonya languishing in a huge bubble bath, a glass of champagne in one hand and a joint in the other.

'Come, come,' she said to me, in what I suppose she imagined was a regal manner, patting the rim of the bath. 'Sit here and talk to Ton-ton.' I got the feeling she didn't want conversation so much as someone to observe her at her queenly ablutions, and I soon learnt to find excuses not to have to 'talk to Ton-ton' while she bathed.

Poor Tonya: I don't think she was entirely right in the head. And things went seriously south for her some weeks later when one of the lowly men she'd spurned took the opportunity, while we were at port in New York, to visit a sex shop there. Paging through the porn magazines on offer, he was thrilled to find one featuring none other than our Tonya, stark naked in a double-page spread, pleasuring another woman. Still smarting from having been given the bum's rush by her, he bought the magazine and wasted no time in photocopying the relevant pages and distributing them all over the ship.

A day later Tonya was found in her bunk, unconscious, with a needle dangling from her arm. Further investigation unearthed a stash of heroin in her cabin. Tonya, the disliked and misunderstood glory-hole steward who also happened to be a heroin addict and a lesbian porn star, was disembarked at the next port.

And then there was Will Moor – a man whose name I remember only because I was forced to.

Will, an inveterate snob, entered my consciousness because of his castle – or, rather, the castle in whose shadow he'd grown up, as he'd tell anyone who stopped long enough to listen. Will's home had been, apparently, a neighbour to the fortification built by William the Conqueror in 1068. It didn't matter to him – or to the American clientele he shamelessly tried to impress with his British pedigree – that Warwick Castle was now owned by the Tussauds Group and operated as a tourist attraction, including such questionable drawcards as 'Warwick, Ghosts Alive' and 'Flight of the Eagles', a bird show.

Until a certain day when I learnt differently, I assumed Will to be just what he appeared: a mousy, rather nondescript little man with somewhat pathetic aspirations to nobility. I found him annoying; once, having heard him cite his lineage to a customer trapped in a chair under an apron, I advised him to 'just shut up and do hairdressing'. In retrospect, that may have been the trigger for what happened subsequently.

It was after we'd sailed into Southampton and gone through our debriefings. At the end of every cruise these debriefings were done by senior management from Steiner, who would come down from London and interview all Steiners who'd been aboard for a feel of what was working, what wasn't, and how they could improve their service. They began with the most junior staff and worked up to the most senior.

As the manager at the time, I went last. I was astonished, on sitting down, to be told that I'd had a 'very serious accusation' levelled against me: sexual harassment.

'My god,' I said. 'By whom?'

Will bloody Moor.

I couldn't help it: I started laughing. 'You can't be serious,' I said.

'Look,' said the interviewer, 'we think we've sorted it out. Ian has told us Will has issues.' Ian Carmichael, who later became the Queen's hairdresser, was Will's cabin mate on this tour, and had been in for his debriefing directly before me.

In spite of, allegedly, being so enthusiastically harassed in a sexual manner by me that he wanted to disembark for good, Will came back aboard for the next cruise. This wasn't a man I would even have noticed if he hadn't spouted endless nonsense about Warwick-effing-Castle, but I'd been given the heads-up by Ian and the supervisor, so on that next world tour I went out of my way to avoid all contact with him.

And yet, about three weeks into that next cruise, I was paid a strangely surreptitious visit by the ship's pharmacist, who poked his head into the salon one afternoon and said, 'Richard, a word, if I may?'

Intrigued, I stepped out into the corridor. The pharmacist palmed me a bottle. 'Wash the affected area twice a day with this,' he murmured, spy-like.

I took the bottle of lotion and read the label. It contained Pyrethrin, a treatment for genital crabs.

'And you think I've got crabs because…?' I said.

The pharmacist looked embarrassed. 'Well, I've just treated your… your friend, and he says his last sexual contact was with you.'

'My "friend" wouldn't happen to be Will Moor, would it?' I asked.

The pharmacist looked relieved. 'Will, yes,' he said. 'So you understand the instructions?'

'I do,' I said, grimly.

I was even more scrupulous about avoiding all contact with Will from that point on. The last I heard of him was that he was on the game in London's Marble Arch.

My brush with Will Moor taught me that hell hath no fury like a queen scorned, so I suppose I should have seen the signs when it happened again. This time, it was with a piss-elegant moffie called Keith, a fellow hairdresser, who – unbeknown to me – moved bureaucratic heaven and earth to secure a double cabin with me as his cabin-mate. I didn't realise that he had the hots for me, and good-naturedly (I thought) brushed off his advances.

At the end of that tour – it was during the winter, when we were doing trans-Atlantic crossings – Keith disembarked. The next time we sailed into Southampton, about days days later, the police were waiting. A covey of customs officials scurried on board, came straight down to the salon and told us that they wanted to search the cabins of all the Steiner men.

Finally, I twigged: Keith. He wasn't a dopehead himself, but he'd watched – with, I realised in retrospect, disapproval –

while Sandra (about whom more later) and I skinned up after duty now and again, going out onto 3 Deck, which was near our cabins, to smoke a spliff.

Well, I had nothing to fear – I had no drugs of any kind in my cabin – so I willingly accompanied two customs officials below decks, and watched while they searched everywhere. And I mean *everywhere*. They emptied cupboards, went through suit pockets, looked in shoes, groped around under my mattress, riffled through photo albums… they even went so far as to pour out my washing powder and squeeze out my toothpaste.

An hour later they finally finished their search. Not surprisingly, they'd come up empty-handed.

'Hey,' I said, as a joke, 'you haven't looked *under* that drawer.'

My bed was a truckle bed, one of those with a big drawer underneath it. The two customs men gave me a skeef look. Then one of them stepped forward, yanked the drawer out, fumbled around behind it… and fuck me if he didn't come out with a bloody stop of dagga!

I think it was very obvious to the customs officials that I was completely gobsmacked. 'Jesus!' I said. 'What's that?'

'This, sir,' said the man holding the stop, 'is marijuana. And it's illegal.'

I burst out laughing. 'You guys don't know how often I've lain in bed here, wishing I had a joint, and all the time there's been dagga right here in my cabin!'

We put the stop on the little bedside table and gently pulled it open. The paper it was wrapped in was from the *QE2*'s events programme, which is printed daily for passengers, and it was dated 1981 – eight years before.

I had to go through the rigmarole of having my passport confiscated while the police labs did their work, but the report came back as we'd all expected it to: the marijuana was very old and clearly hadn't been stashed in the cabin by me.

That night, while I was sitting in the Midships Bar having an after-work drink, the head of ship security happened to come in. 'Hey, Bob,' I said, 'did you hear what happened to me today?'

'Yup,' he said. 'And let me tell you two things. One, whenever you're assigned a new cabin, or come back to your old cabin after you've been on leave, search every inch of it – you never know what some idiot has left behind. And, two, thank your lucky stars that this happened in England.

There are places in the world where just the presence of that dope in your cabin would have got you locked away for life.'

§

A crew member whose heart was unfalteringly in the right place – with his fiancée – was one of our cruise sales managers, a remarkably goodlooking man called Martin, who I took a serious fancy to despite his being firmly straight. He'd left his fiancée in New York City and had made a pact with her that he would have sex of no kind – including masturbation – until he returned after the 96-day cruise and could share the experience with her.

Martin and I spent a lot of time together – me lusting fruitlessly after him, him making sure to fulfil his other promise to his beloved fiancée, that of buying her a doll from every city the ship visited.

Once, in Pattaya in Thailand, when Martin and I decided to stay off the ship overnight and booked a hotel room together, I thought my luck might be in – the room had only a double bed. Unfortunately, another Steiner employee, a woman called Wendy, joined us in Pattaya and, having missed the last launch back the ship, ended up sharing the bed with us – sleeping between us! I never really liked Wendy again after that, and was secretly thrilled when she put on so much weight she had to surreptitiously let out her uniform so that the Steiner higher-ups wouldn't realise she was getting too fat for the job.

Martin married his fiancée when he returned from the world cruise and, as far as I know, they lived happily ever after.

§

We called passengers 'bloods', for reasons I don't know; and difficult passengers were 'bad bloods'. Bad bloods were those who were stupidly pernickety or just inconsiderate when it came to cabin service. The cabin stewards were required to hover in the shadows each morning until the occupants of the eight cabins in each of their stewardships emerged and went off for breakfast; then they would swoop in, silent and speedy, and put all to rights. Beds were made up with pristine linen; towels were changed; clothes were folded or hung up; surfaces were buffed; carpets were vacuumed; and, as a final touch, toilet rolls were given that artful little arrow-fold in their ends.

One of the 1 Deck stewards, Jim, had the misfortune to have under his care a Japanese passenger whose tastes were so particular, whose demands so precise, that Jim was very close to breaking point by a week into the world cruise. Not only was this unspeakable person – whom we called The Tyrant – never satisfied with a single thing, he was also infuriatingly inconsiderate when it came to shore leave.

Of course, I'm not suggesting that the *QE2*'s high-paying passengers should have had anything but the most passing regard for the minions who attended to their every need, but most of our guests quickly cottoned on to how important it was, when we docked in some or other port, to get moving at a reasonable hour of the morning. Not only did this work for them – there was so much to see, so much to do, so much money to spend – but for the cabin stewards, who were similarly itching for shore leave, it was vital. Before they were allowed ashore, the stewards had to scrupulously clean every square millimetre of the cabins under their care, so getting their bloods up and moving as early as politely possible was pretty important. (When at sea, passengers lazing late in bed wasn't a problem for the cabin stewards; there was, after all, nowhere else for anyone to go.)

The Tyrant, however, didn't give a rat's arse about the crew (or anyone else, for that matter), and when Jim had finished up his other seven cabins and his difficult guest was still abed at 11am when practically everyone else on board had gone ashore in Honolulu, he vacuumed furiously outside in the corridor, singing loud yodelling songs and banging madly on the walls to try to wake up his tardy guest. Finally – finally! – The Tyrant emerged. He snapped a few angry words at Jim and marched off down the corridor to find himself a leisurely brunch.

Jim looked at his watch and guesstimated how long it would take him to straighten up The Tyrant's stateroom. He wasn't a neat man, and Jim realised, with a sinking heart, that his 'watch off' was almost over and there wasn't a prayer he'd get finished in time to go ashore. With helpless frustration, he spent a vigorous half-hour changing linen, dusting, polishing and vacuuming. In the bathroom, he swabbed down the shower, washed out the sink, replaced the towels and mopped the floor. Then, grabbing the toilet brush, he opened the toilet bowl to give it its regulation scrub.

There, stuck to the inside like a gift from the gods, was a pea-sized speck of turd.

Jim didn't hesitate. He snatched The Tyrant's toothbrush from out of the silver-plated holder and, kneeling down, used the toothbrush to delicately flick the tiny bit of crap into the water. He replaced the toothbrush, used the toilet brush to scrub the lavatory, and put the toilet seat down with the satisfied air of a job well done.

§

While most *QE2* staff had to make do with shared, cramped cabins, there were those who had relatively salubrious accommodation. Managers and assistant managers had, for instance, a cabin to themselves, with an en suite bathroom – a big step up from the joint accommodations and, worse, shared ablutions of more menial staff, and one that could only be truly appreciated once you'd had a shower together with a bucketful of fish heads, the communal showers being where the Filipino staff stashed this 'delicacy'.

A staff member who was lucky enough to have passenger accommodation was Liesel, the onboard representative for American Express. I remember her for a wild party we had in her cabin, which started onshore in Bermuda and ended up almost getting me fired.

t was the late 1980s, and the National Union of Seamen – up to that point, the principal trade union of merchant seafarers in the UK – had just disbanded prior to its amalgamation with the National Union of Railwaymen to form the National Union of Rail, Maritime and Transport Workers. For various reasons, this was to forever change the nature and makeup of the crew of the *QE2* and at the time there was an end-of-days feeling on board, so when we were granted shore leave in Bermuda, a group of us, including myself, Liesel, Tony and Ray Jones, and two other waiters, hit the town with a vengeance.

We crowded into a downtown pub called The Cock and Feather and ordered a round of Mother's Milk, a potent cocktail made up of white, black and gold rum, Triple Sec, apricot brandy and banana liqueur, topped off with a touch of fruit juice and served in a pint glass. Then we ordered another round and another and so on, until each of us had paid for a round – by which time, each of us sloshing with six pints of Mother's Milk, we were motherless.

I can't remember much of what happened subsequently as we roamed, hysterical with drunkenness, around Bermuda, although I do recall us shamelessly – and illegally – using our crew passes to board another ship in the harbour, the *Homeric*, where we gaily stripped naked and went skinny-dipping in the pool.

Finally, around 2am, we realised that we were in danger of missing the last launch back out to the *QE2* (which would have meant not being in time to report for work the next morning, an unforgivable offence). We made it, probably not least because the launch itself came in late. By the time it arrived, I was wholly incapable of independent motion, and was carried aboard by a friendly colleague in a fireman's lift.

At 45 minutes, the ferry out of Bermuda harbour and back to the ship was an unusually long one for a *QE2* tender, so we had plenty of time to behave in a really silly manner. En route, we were tantalised beyond reason by the empty flagpole at the back of the launch. 'We need a flag!' Liesel screamed madly, before whipping off her red G-string and tying it to the pole. We all thought this a terrific idea, and before long the flagpole was fluttering with our underwear – some red jockies, a white bra, a blue camisole.

Back on board, with renewed feelings of indestructibility, we repaired, along with several other crew members we picked up along the way, to Liesel's cabin to continue the party.

It was 4am when two security men banged on the cabin door – they'd had several complaints from passengers in nearby cabins. For reasons I don't recall, I was under Liesel's bed, dressed only in a towelling robe and wearing an ice bucket on my head. 'Where are you supposed to be?' one of the security men asked me sternly when I poked my nose out.

'Me? I live here,' I slurred, happily. (To be fair to me, I wasn't telling a flat-out lie: I did occasionally share Liesel's relatively luxurious accommodation, sleeping in one of her twin beds.)

'Get out!' ordered the security man and I, dazed with alcoholic cheer, wandered down off down the corridor, still wearing my robe and my ice bucket.

The next morning I woke up with the most astonishing hangover and reported for duty at the salon. My manageress, Jen, wasn't there: I discovered that she was in the captain's office, trying to keep my job for me. Liesel had already been fired; not only had news of the party got back to the captain, but several passengers on the last launch we'd taken to get back to the ship the previous night had complained that some staff members, riotous with intoxication, had urinated on them. (Of that, I have absolutely no memory; I do think it's possible that the removal of our underwear for the purposes of decorating the empty flagpole caused the passengers – no doubt outraged, and with reason, by our behaviour – to draw fanciful conclusions.)

Jen really went to bat for me, demanding, if I was fired, that the four waiters and all the other people who'd been at the party should also be identified and dismissed. The pow-wow in the captain's office went on for several hours and in the end Jen saved my job.

As part of my punishment, I had to write a letter of apology to the captain, which I still have. Addressed to Staff Captain Carr, it read, 'Please accept my apologies regarding the incidents that happened on the night of 17 September. I frankly was not aware I was not permitted to be in another concessionaire's cabin. Also, although I was enjoying myself ashore, I did not consider my behaviour to be unruly or offensive. I am grateful for your final decision that I am to continue duties with Steiner on the Queen Elizabeth 2.'

It was, even if I say so myself, an exercise in talking around the point. I didn't mention what I'd been wearing in Liesel's cabin or where I'd been found there; and 'enjoying myself ashore' was a wonderwork of understatement.

When I went to deliver the letter, the staff captain was actually very decent. 'Richard,' he explained, taking the letter from me, 'you must understand that in a situation like this, forewarned is forearmed. If I'd known what had gone on last night and knew I was going to be dealing with passengers' complaints this morning, I might have been able to handle things differently.'

I took his advice to heart. Two months later, in Tenerife, I went on another bender, this time with a crew member called Frank. After a night of intense merry-making, we decided we were hungry and found a taxi-driver willing to take us somewhere for food. Again, my memory of the night is somewhat blurry, but I do recall shouting, 'Manger! Manger!' (French for 'Eat! Eat!', which was probably not very useful, since Tenerife, part of the Canary Islands, is Spanish) at the taxi driver, who drove us an unseemly distance to buy food that, had we been sober, we would doubtless have found inedible.

Our appetites satisfied, we instructed the taxi driver to take us back to the harbour, where Frank hopped out and nipped up the gangway of the ship, leaving me to negotiate the fare.

'One hundred twenty-five dollar,' the taxi driver said, holding out a hand.

Even in my drunken state I knew I was being had – $125 was a fortune in Tenerife in those days – and I said, 'Fuck off, I'm not paying that.'

The taxi driver lunged for me and I, rendered once again indestructible by alcohol, scarpered cheekily up the gangway. The taxi driver ran after me, rugby-tackling me and, once he had me down, clawing at my ankles. Giggling maniacally, I kicked him off and dragged my way up the gangway into the safety of the ship.

The next morning I realised I might once again be in some trouble, so I went straight to the staff captain and, remembering his advice about forewarned being forearmed, told him what I'd done. He shrugged – the incident hadn't disturbed any passengers, he said, so he didn't really care. 'I'd just advise you not to go ashore today,' he said, giving my arm a friendly pat. 'You don't want to be jumped by an angry taxi driver and his mates.'

I could hardly believe, after having come so close to losing my job just two months before, that I'd got off so lightly – but the staff captain wasn't finished with me yet. Later that day he phoned me in the salon. 'Richard, we have a problem,' he said, his voice grim.

My heart sank. 'What?' I asked.

'What you did last night has caused something of an international incident – stiffing the locals, lack of respect for customs, that sort of thing. We've been told the *QE2* isn't going to be allowed to dock here in the future.'

'Jesus,' I breathed, my legs going weak under me. 'Fuck. What should I do?'

Then he started laughing, the bastard. 'Got you!' he said. 'Next time, just pay the bloody taxi driver.'

(Neither of these incidents is a patch on what happened on the *QE2* at the end of the 2005 world cruise – after my time

– when some crew members went on a rampage after an onboard crew party. Among the damages were furniture, fittings and artwork, and a unique tapestry, specially commissioned for the launch of the ship, was thrown overboard. Needless to say, there were plenty firings following that misbehaviour.)

4. The Cabins

A ticket on the *QE2*, even the cheapest one, cost what most people would consider a modest fortune. For the exceptionally well heeled it may have been small change; but for some of the merely very rich, the purchase price of the ticket was only to get them on board – after that, it was up to their own ingenuity to get upgraded as much and as often as they possibly could.

We learned to recognise these people as they came up the gangway – it wasn't difficult; they were the ones already rumbling with discontent. Over the first few days of the cruise, they would find any number of things wrong with their bought-and-paid-for accommodation on the less-than-salubrious 5 Deck – they were berthed next to a crew member; their bedside light didn't work or their toilet didn't flush properly; the tug hit their porthole window at some ungodly hour of the night and woke them up… The complaints were as varied as they were many.

And, sooner or later, the purser would be forced to concede defeat, and upgrade the moaning minnies to more expensive accommodation. And with this upgrade in stateroom came several perks – one of them being that your stateroom dictated which of the four restaurants you ate in, and the more expensive your stateroom, the better the restaurant you were allocated.

But these cheapskates tripped themselves up in all sorts of ways. One was a woman who complained that her 'Versace gown' had been stolen. Designer gowns were part and parcel of most passengers' luggage – they would come on board in huge hanging boxes, and be carefully stowed and as carefully tended to by the cabin stewards.

A single gown could cost many thousands of dollars, so obviously the purser was greatly concerned about this theft. He immediately sat the distraught woman down and asked her for some details. 'And where did you last see your Versace gown, madam?' he asked.

'It was in the tumble-dryer,' she said, wringing her hands.

'In the *tumble-dryer*, madam?' the purser asked, not bothering to hide his astonishment.

'Yes, I'd just given it a quick machine-wash and stuck it in the tumble-dryer…' the woman explained.

The purser closed his notebook. 'We'll keep an eye out for it, madam,' he said, not intending to do any such thing.

A cheapskate passenger once took off her earrings while I styled her hair and then forgot to take them with her when she left. I put them in a drawer, intending to return them when I saw her again, but as it happened, the cruise ended shortly afterwards and I didn't get the opportunity.

A month later, I cleaned out my drawers and threw the earrings away. As luck would have it, the very same day the security officer came to the salon. 'A passenger has written to complain that she left behind some extremely valuable earrings,' he said. 'She's threatening to sue if we don't return them. She says they're worth $250 000.'

'I know exactly what earrings she's talking about, and if she paid $25 for them, she was ripped off,' I said. 'I've thrown them away.'

The security officer shrugged. 'It's your word against hers. You'd better find them.'

I dispatched two members of my staff down to the ship's recycling plant where, fortunately, they were able to locate the black rubbish bag I'd filled the day before. They scratched through it and came up with the earrings – which were, indeed, nothing but cheap tat. I wiped them off, wrapped them very carefully in tissue paper and mailed them back to the passenger. I'd like to believe she had a moment of deep embarrassment when she got them, but I've learned that some people are simply impossible to shame.

It was just as well, however, that that incident occurred after the ship had had its recycling plant installed. It seems astonishing now, when we go to such great lengths to dispose responsibly of our waste, but prior to that, every bit of garbage produced by the liner was simply hefted overboard. Up until the late 1980s, the daily leavings of almost three thousand people (1 800 passengers and just over 1 000 crew) were packed into black plastic bags and thrown into the sea. Plastic, paper, foodstuffs, metal, glass – no matter what it was, it got jettisoned.

I'd chucked those cheap and nasty earrings away, but when passengers left behind more valuable articles, these were taken to Lost Property. The crew member who handed them in left their name and, three months later, if the property hadn't been reclaimed by the person who'd lost it, it defaulted to the crew member who'd found it. By this simple expedient, I am today the proud owner of four Armani jerseys, two pairs of diamond earrings (the real deal, these ones), a beautiful overcoat, and several other garments and items of jewellery that I otherwise would never have been able to afford to own.

Of course, not all the not-so-madly-wealthy were cheapskates. The ones who really broke my heart were the wives whose husbands had brought them on a *QE2* world cruise and who couldn't get over how lucky they were to have a spouse of such vision and largesse. One in particular – I'll call her Mrs Jones – told me repeatedly how her husband valued and spoiled her. They'd been married for 35 years, she said, and he still treated her like a queen. Hadn't he brought her on this astonishingly expensive holiday? Didn't he allow – nay, encourage! – her to come to the salon every evening around 7pm for a relaxing, luxurious wash and blow? What a generous husband he was, how understanding, how lucky she was to be married to such a fine, fine man!

But I knew something that Mrs Jones didn't (because – and make no mistake about this – a ship's crew, like a hotel's staff, know everything that's worth knowing about their clients): that Mr Jones had an assignation of his own every evening at 7pm, in the spa hot pool, with any male crew member who was willing. While the sadly clueless but eternally grateful Mrs Jones was getting a blow from me, Mr Jones was getting one from one of my colleagues.

And there were the 'ordinary' people who travelled on the *QE2*, for whom the cruise was a once-in-a-lifetime experience. In the case of my friend Verna, who now (coincidentally) lives near me, it was a commemoration of an unusual kind: she and her newly ex husband took the cruise when they divorced after 15 years of marriage and two children, to celebrate their amicable parting of ways.

Verna, who's now in her 60s, remembers her ex-husband's wicked sense of humour coming into play when, strolling past people putting together one of the hundreds of jigsaw puzzles provided for passengers, would lean sideways and say, *sotto voce*, 'You do know there's a piece missing, don't you?'

Another South African cruiser of 'ordinary' means was Mrs Van der Walt, a nasty snob who, when discussing with me the doings and screwings of her fellow passengers while in the chair, would turn up her nose in distaste and sniff, 'Ja, Richard: soort soek soort, nê?' (Afrikaans for 'birds of a feather flock together'.) I always found it rather odd to have these strangely parochial little Afrikaans chats with Mrs Van der Walt on the *QE2*, surrounded as we were by largely sophisticated folk of many other nationalities.

I remember Mrs Van der Walt for three idiosyncrasies: one, she embarked and disembarked in New York, and never once, *ever*, during the entire journey of the ship around the planet, got off *anywhere* else; two, her hair was thinning to the extent that she required a 'comb-over', more common among South African men of her vintage; and, three (and most annoying, for me), she would use the time the ship spent in any port to have her hair done – and never before 11am, which more than once scuppered my chances for shore leave and made me inclined to comb her hair out just a little more enthusiastically than I would with other passengers.

Another was a dear old thing called Eve Goodie, another Dame Edna Everage lookalike whose hair simply couldn't be big enough. She'd come in for a wash and set, and after I'd taken the rollers out, I'd spend some time teasing her hair up into a wild halo until it looked as if she'd just had ten thousand volts shot through her. Then I'd put down my comb, brush off my hands and walk away. 'There, darling, you're done!' I'd say.

Eve loved this. 'Richard!' she'd squeal. 'Come back!'

And so I would, and there would follow an immensely intricate process that involved smoothing, spraying, more teasing, more smoothing and yet more spraying. Eve *loved* hairspray.

Once, the salon was very busy. I'd almost finished with Eve but had to leave her for a few moments to attend to another client's needs, and Eve didn't like that – 'Richard!' she called petulantly. 'You haven't sprayed me yet!'

Eve was a beloved regular, so I pointed behind me to the shelf that held the hair products and said, 'There's the can. Take it down and give yourself a few squirts.'

What I hadn't realised was that the hairspray was right next to the hair mousse, and that the two were in similar cans. When I next turned around, dear old Eve had all but disappeared under a mound of white fluff; she looked like a snowman.

She hadn't looked at herself in the mirror yet, so I quickly whipped her into a chair, briskly removed the mountainous swirls of mousse, and applied liberal lashings of hairspray. Eve was delighted and her 'do, shored up by the mousse, stayed perfectly in place for the next two weeks.

Another set of folk aboard who weren't wealthy but were nonetheless extraordinary were the 350 9th Air Force Association veterans of 'D-Day', the June 1944 invasion of Normandy, France during the Second World War during which 37 000 people were killed. These intrepid old men – among them comedian Bob Hope and legendary US radio and TV journalist Walter Cronkite, who gave eye-witness accounts of the invasion – did the trans-Atlantic crossing on the *QE2* in 1994 from New York to Southampton. Many of them had sailed the same route on the original *Queen Elizabeth* when it was refitted for war in the early 1940s.

The anniversary journey took a week, at the end of which the *QE2* led a flotilla of ships that were reviewed by Queen Elizabeth II, Prince Philip and other world leaders. Then it crossed the English Channel and anchored off the Normandy beaches on 6 June, the exact day fifty years later that the Normandy landings had begun. There, the ship sent out 'V for Victory' (three dots and a dash) messages throughout the day. Dame Vera Lynn, then 77 years old, the most popular British singer of World War II ballads and known as 'The Forces' Sweetheart', performed her repertory including her very famous 'White Cliffs of Dover'.

Many of these sad and saggy old men (some of whom proudly wore their original, worn-out uniforms and medals) had photographs of their 50-years-younger selves with them, which they eagerly showed to anyone who might take the time to look. In these snapshots they were so attractive – young and vital, their bodies strong and their faces seemingly lit from within with the loveliness of youth.

It was a salutary reminder of the fleeting nature of both youth and beauty – an interesting notion for me to ponder as a young gay man obsessed with the apparent importance of good looks.

But more recently Vera Lynn showed that age (and, her in case, great age) doesn't necessarily have anything to do with popularity. *We'll Meet Again: The Very Best of Vera Lynn*, a compilation album, was released in 2009 to coincide with the 70th anniversary of the outbreak of the war. At age 92, Vera shot up the British album charts to take second place by August 2009, behind hugely popular British band Arctic Monkeys but ahead of globe-trotting French DJ David Guetta and US rockers Kings of Leon. This made her the oldest living artist to have a number-two hit – 70 years after the release of her first wartime classic, 'We'll Meet Again'.

5. The Penthouses

The *QE2* wasn't originally built with penthouse suites; these – twenty of them – were only added in 1972, on Signal Deck and Sun Deck, behind the ship's bridge. In 1977 two more penthouse suites were added – these ones with balconies, making the *QE2* one of the first ships to have private terraces. And in 1986, during a major refit, another eight were built on.

There were passengers who thought nothing of spending hundreds of thousands of pounds for this prime accommodation on the *QE2*'s world cruises. For these regulars, the liner became a home-away-from-home on which they would spend four months of each year.

One of these was Mr Goldberg, a ghastly name-dropper who had, after his wife passed away, married her nurse – in fact, he and the nurse had come onto the ship at Fort Lauderdale and got married on board; I was responsible for the hair for that wedding.

Over eight of the years I worked on the *QE2*, Mr Goldberg forked out for *eight* penthouses every year – for himself, his wife and his business manager. I once asked the second

Mrs Goldberg why they needed eight penthouses for just the three of them. 'Well,' she said, 'we have a castle on the Isle of Wight and a mansion in Florida, so we're used to a lot of space. And if we didn't have all this room,' she said, sweeping an arm out to indicate the £100 000-odd worth of accommodation her husband had rented, 'we'd probably start feeling a little claustrophobic.'

This putative claustrophobia didn't stop the Goldbergs – whom we called 'Lord and Lady QE2' – filling their penthouses from floor to ceiling with purchases from all over the world. Wherever the ship put in to port, the Goldbergs would go on a massive shopping spree, and over the four months their cabins filled up with some of the most expensive and beautiful products the world had to offer: silks, furniture, statuary, paintings, carpets… if it was gorgeous and cost the earth, they bought it.

(Although on a much, much smaller scale, we crew members also enjoyed buying mementoes of our global travels. Early in my time on the *QE2* I decided I'd stick to a theme for each of my world cruises, so came home each time with a range of, say, boxes or owls or picture frames or plates. Once my theme was pigs and I was delighted to find, in a monastery village in Bali, a beautiful cast-iron porker. Bali was a great destination for tourist tat and you could trade cheap items like ballpoint pens, bars of soap and towels for just about anything your heart desired; but this particular craftsman had set a price to his pigs – $35 – and wouldn't accept anything lower or other. I refused to pay such a ridiculous sum but even as the ship was leaving the port I was already missing that pig, and a year later, when we returned to Bali on the next world cruise, I made my way straight back to the same monastery village – and found the same cast-iron pigs for sale, still at the same price. This time, I bought one – but it was promptly taken off me on my return to Cape Town by my good friend Carl, who fell in love with it as thoroughly as I had, and who displayed it for some years in pride of place on his mantelpiece. No matter – on our next visit to Bali the following year I bought another one – still selling at the same price! – and some time later, Carl returned the original pig to me, so I now have two of them.)

But back to the Goldbergs… The second Mrs Goldberg, despite being married to a man of obscene wealth, had never really become accustomed to the high life. She was shy, and didn't like to come to the salon; instead, I would go to her penthouse every Tuesday and Friday to style her hair. There, I discovered that, in spite of having her choice of the most delectable foods prepared by some of the best chefs, she preferred to make her own breakfast and lunch – and usually something very simple, like a bowl of muesli or a boiled egg on toast. For this purpose, she brought on board with her a range of the most fabulous kitchen equipment – and at the end of each world cruise, she would present me with a box of used (but only barely) silverware, glassware, cutlery and crockery. I still have a lovely pepper-grinder she gave me, and every time I use it, I think of Mrs Goldberg.

Mr Goldberg, for his part, was simply terrified of change. This had the interesting spin-off, for we crew who had to put up with his pernicketiness, of practically guaranteeing our jobs for as long as Mr Goldberg sailed. It was rumoured that if any of the staff Mr Goldberg had become accustomed to on his previous world cruises were changed, he would seriously consider taking berths on another boat.

Mr Goldberg was very specific about how he wanted his hair – if, after a session in my chair, anyone had said to him, 'Nice haircut, Mr Goldberg,' he quite likely would have fired me. My brief was simple but exacting: Mr Goldberg's hair was always to look precisely the same.

Mr Goldberg would book his weekly appointments with me a year in advance – he had the 10am slot every Thursday, for an invisible trim-and-style, and a manicure. He would sweep into the salon at 10 on the dot, and he required that I was always ready, holding his chair out for him, and that the manicurist was so placed that as he sat down, his hands would land in hers, ready to be pampered.

Mr Goldberg wasn't shy about his requirements. If he wanted, for instance, to pop into the Midships Bar for an evening cocktail with his wife, he would phone ahead and tell the manager that he was coming. A prime table would be selected and reserved – but all the tables surrounding that table would also be cleared and reserved. Mr Goldberg didn't like being too close to people who were mere mortals.

Once this happened when another paying passenger happened to be in the bar. The passenger watched, amazed, while Lord and Lady QE2 sailed in, seated themselves in their cleared and reserved space with staff fussing around them like busy little tugboats, had a pina colada apiece, then sailed out again. 'What have they got that I haven't?' he asked in astonishment.

I didn't answer him but I'd have thought it was obvious: lots and lots and *lots* of money.

As a 'regular' on the Goldbergs' *QE2* staff list, I was handsomely rewarded, and pocketed a $100 tip each Thursday from Mr Goldberg and another hundred on the Friday from his wife. Proving, however, that money can't buy love, this didn't endear me at all to Mr Goldberg.

(Although our wages on the *QE2* were disgracefully low, the tips were good. An Irish colleague gave me some good advice early in my career: to wear a shirt with a breast pocket, and to put a dollar bill in it at the beginning of each day. This worked in an interesting 'like attracts like' way, and it was rare that I didn't have $100 in tips in that pocket by the end of the day. Towards the end of my time on the *QE2* I was regularly making between $400 and $800 a day in tips – but, make no mistake, I was seriously licking arse for that.)

When it came to Mr Goldberg, what did cheer me up – and what thoroughly wiped the smile from his face – was when his juvenile-delinquent daughter joined the ship to spend some time with her father. Goldberg Junior was a drug-addled piece of work who boasted every personality disorder known to psychiatry and probably a few besides. Depending on her state of mind and her father's tolerance levels, she would spend anything from two weeks to two months making Mr Goldberg's life a misery. Needless to say, she was a favourite with the crew.

As if money breeds madness, there were always eccentrics on board. One was a charming but totally batty old dear, Mrs Macky, who regularly took two 1 Deck staterooms on the world cruises – one for herself and one for her vast collection of stuffed animals, which were as real and alive to her as anyone else's flesh-and-blood pets. There were close on a hundred of these fluffy toys, and each was individually dressed in a beautiful, hand-sewn outfit.

Mrs Macky was scrupulous about giving each of her 'pets' individual attention, and could be seen with a different one at various times of the day – the stuffed bunny, for instance, would accompany her to breakfast; the toy bear would require its own seat next to her in the salon while we did her hair; a fluffy kitten would join her at lunch; a kangaroo, pert in a miniature Aussie bush hat complete with corks, was her companion at afternoon tea; and a wiry dog with lolling felt tongue would perch next to her at dinner. 'They get lonely without me,' she would tell us, solemnly. 'They need a lot of love and care.' Dear Mrs Macky, it was clear that she was the one in need – if not of love and care, then at least a bit of light electric shock therapy.

Another two who favoured stuffed animals were Diane and Ken Jenking-Rees, frequent cruisers, who travelled with a toy camel called Cedric and a teddy-bear called Little Ted – both of which had Platinum Guest status. Of course, these passengers were gently indulged, and once Cedric and Little Ted were actually introduced at a welcoming party.

Interestingly, I discovered during my time on the *QE2* that even the super-wealthy aren't immune to petty theft now and again (or perhaps it was plain old kleptomania). Once a female passenger, dripping with gold and diamonds, asked if she could use the salon to try on a top she'd bought. I thought nothing of it and said of course. After she emerged and scuttled off, I discovered that my vent brush (a specialised piece of equipment for brushing out hair) was missing.

The ship lost countless thousands of pounds worth of *QE2*- or Cunard-branded goods during its cruises – crockery that 'fell into' people's luggage, salt and pepper pots that disappeared from tables (I still have a set!), linen that walked… shrinkage was a given. In fact, earlier on in my career, there were nifty little 'sign holders' in all the public corridors and rooms, with removable branded *QE2* notices that informed passengers of vital information, for instance 'clocks will be advanced/retarded by one hour at midnight tonight'. A couple of years in and these sign-holders had all been removed: the notices were nicked by passengers the minute they were inserted into the sign-holders, and the practice had, of necessity, to be discontinued.

Another passenger who had more money than God was a woman called Heidi. Her marvellous generosity was mirrored in her body shape – she was one of the largest women I've ever met. (I heard she eventually she had her stomach stapled to try to get her weight down.)

Heidi was always accompanied by her husband, Neville – a scrawny stick-figure of a man who spent much of his time literally in his wife's shadow. Heidi would sweep into a room on board and look around for her husband; not seeing him, she would roar, 'Neville!' and this tiny little man would step out from behind her. 'Yes, dear?' he would say, mildly.

When she came on board, Heidi would pay visits to all the staff who would be looking after her for the next few months and ask them what gift they would like her to give them when the cruise ended – she didn't want to buy them something they didn't want or would never use.

One year, when she asked me, I told her I'd like one of those eight-foot-tall wooden carved giraffes that were all the rage at the time. Heidi thought this a fine idea, and added that she had 'some friends' in Florida who would probably like to receive the same gift.

The 'some' friends turned out to number 22, and when we put in at Mombasa in Kenya, Heidi excitedly went ashore to seek her giraffes. She duly found them, and that evening 23 strapping young Kenyan men marched up the gangway, each carrying an eight-foot-tall wooden giraffe. Twenty-two of these were stowed in Heidi and Neville's penthouse; Heidi gave me mine.

Neville was just short enough to be more or less at eye-level with the undercarriage of the gigantic giraffes, and it was this tiny man who pointed out to his wife something that might cause some of their Florida friends embarrassment: all the giraffes were male, and all had an intricately carved wooden penis.

So the next morning, 22 strapping young Kenyan men marched up the gangway once again, and left the same way, each carrying an eight-foot-tall wooden giraffe. And that evening, they returned, each carrying an eight-foot-tall wooden giraffe – each with its penis carefully removed.

(Only 22 of the giraffes got the Bobbitt treatment because I opted to keep my giraffe with its penis intact.)

One gift I didn't – inexplicably – get was from Aziz Ojjeh, the obscenely wealthy co-owner, with his brother Mansour, of TAG Holdings. The Ojjeh brothers, whose business was instrumental in the revival of the Heuer watch company (which became known as TAG-Heuer), were involved in Formula 1 racing (Mansour spent about $5 million to pay Porsche to design and build TAG turbo engines for Grand Prix racing), in the selling and leasing of executive jets, and in property development, agriculture and banking – so there was absolutely no shortage of money there.

But, from my point of view anyway, there was certainly a shortage of attention to detail. During one of the world cruises, Aziz and his wife distributed among the crew

TAG-Heuer brochures of the latest big-ticket watches, many of them retailing for several thousands of dollars, and invited everyone, as a present from them, to make a selection.

Everyone, that is, except me.

The Ojjehs went ashore in Singapore to collect the designer watches and I watched in mute disbelief as all the staff who'd looked after them on their trip – everyone from cabin stewards to waiters, gym instructors to managers – received their gifts.

I didn't stay mute for long. I was furious. *Where was mine? Why had I been overlooked??* My rich-as-Croesus friend Sue-Anne (a frequent cruiser, about whom more later) listened to me rant and rail, and she sympathised with me. She had her own reasons to be irritated with the Ojjehs: their travelling companion, a rather dirty-looking little fellow who played heavily on the fact of his friendship with the wealthy couple, had invited Sue-Anne back to his cabin and, when Sue-Anne declined to accept his offer of 'some Arab sausage', had become aggressive, forcing her to fight her way out of what was quickly becoming a nasty encounter.

'Don't worry, darling,' she said. 'I'll buy you one.'

I grumpily accepted her kind offer – but it wasn't the actual absence of a pricey watch I resented, it was the snub of being left off the gift list.

Sue-Anne did buy me a TAG-Heuer watch shortly afterwards. I'm delighted to report that the bloody thing has never kept proper time.

§

A super-wealthy passenger the crew loved to hate was Florence Beet, a person of such dreadful disposition that by the end of the world cruise she would inevitably be getting hate mail pushed under her cabin door. This witch of a woman would, in preparation for joining the world cruise, fly from her home in Los Angeles to meet the boat in New York.

There, she would sit down with a team of interior decorators who would have brought with them suitcases of fabric swatches and samples, and from these Florence would determine the décor of her penthouse, from carpets and curtains to linen and furnishings. In return, she would leave a dozen framed photographs of her nearest-and-dearests, to be incorporated to best effect into the overall design.

Two weeks later, when the ship docked in Los Angeles and Florence got on, she would be shown to her fully refurbished penthouse – tricked out down to the very last detail in furnishings and finishes of Florence's own choosing, and topped off with family photographs that would make the spoilt old brat feel right at home.

This is not to say, of course, that Florence had any taste – like many super-rich, she had more money than sense. Once, when I was styling her hair for a St Patrick's Day cocktail party, I asked what she'd be wearing – the theme was 'a touch of green'. 'My little black Chanel and my emeralds,' she answered.

When I saw her later, all gussied up and ready to join the party, I wondered what she'd thought 'a touch' meant – her 'little black Chanel' was a study in over-the-topness with its eye-boggling green polka dots, and as for her emeralds, well, she was wearing *all* of them. You could hardly see her beneath the glitter-fest of tiara, earrings, necklaces, brooches, rings and bracelets. 'It looks like the emerald bird flew past and shat all over her,' a colleague whispered to me.

Florence was also tremendously vain – something that few people can be with their hairstylists, who're usually privy to all their narcissistic little secrets. One year she didn't make it for the world cruise as she'd got cancer and had to undergo chemotherapy (and I'm sorry to say that when the crew heard she wasn't going to make it on board that year, a huge whoop of joy rang out from prow to stern).

By the time she returned the following year, her hair, which she'd lost as a result of the chemo, had grown back in – but in its natural grey colour. Florence, 'forgetting' that I'd been colouring her hair for years, pointed this out to me. 'Isn't this strange?' she said. 'The chemo turned my hair grey.'

§

Marie Rattray, the wife of a man who'd made his fortune in insurance, was another big spender. She'd arrive on the *QE2* with four carry-on wardrobes; in the 109 days we spent at sea on a world cruise, she never appeared twice in the same outfit.

Marie, who would dearly have loved her husband to be faithful to her (but he wasn't; tragically for Marie, he expired atop his mistress in New York City, and it became Marie's distressing and distasteful task to leave the *QE2* mid-cruise to go and claim his body), fell into a trap that many Women

Of A Certain Age did. Widows and disappointed wives and lifetime spinsters would come on board intent on a once-in-a-lifetime liner love affair – and, for some reason, almost all of them would target the same man (there were, obviously, a limited number of single, available men to be had).

This led to terrible spats between competing women, often in public, and the arguments – some hissed, some rather louder – would almost always come down to money.

One of the most demeaning put-downs I overhead during a nasty 'he's-mine-no-he's-mine' squabble – with the man in question present – was when one wealthy widow turned to the squirming object of both her and her rival's desire and sniffed, 'She's a lady on a budget.'

An icy silence fell. It was not a put-down that the contender could challenge, and she turned and left the room, utterly defeated.

Marie, who was in her 60s but had taken full advantage of the wide range of body-enhancing surgical options on offer, had considerable success with men on the boat. Her reason? 'I've got big tits and a tight fanny.' I suppose some things you just know.

Marie had towering stacks of impressive jewellery which I obviously took to be genuine but which I was told by her daughter, Janine (who visited the ship from time to time; and who, with a kind of humour seldom seen among the rich and tasteless, called herself 'The Hairless Heiress' because she was getting a bit sparse up on top), were mainly paste. Still, I knew Marie had real jewels too, for the simple reason that I smuggled a couple for her.

On one of the world cruises she bought some very rare natural pearls in Japan and a star emerald in Sri Lanka that she didn't want to declare, so I put them in my fanny pack and took them through customs for her (ship's crew was seldom searched in those days).

Marie met me in the Anchor Bar (known to *QE2* crew, probably predictably, as the Wanker Bar) on the land side of New York harbour to reclaim her loot and gave me $100 for my trouble – an extremely modest commission for smuggling several million dollars' worth of jewellery past officialdom.

(Poor Marie: in her quest for the slenderness of youth, she bought into the 'fen-phen' craze that swept the world in the 1990s. A combination of the appetite-suppressant prescription drugs fenfluramine and phentermine was guaranteed to melt away the pounds – but also caused serious heart-valve problems. The FDA ban on fenfluramine in 1997 didn't come soon enough for Marie, who died of a heart attack.)

The Wanker Bar was a staple for us on arriving and leaving New York City. It was an eclectic place that fulfilled all sorts of needs – it had a bank of phones, vital in those pre-cellphone days for contacting home; it sold everything from condoms and diet pills to bedding and underwear; it had a good, cheapish restaurant that appreciated its regulars (I'd invariably be greeted, on arrival, with a shouted, 'Hey, Japie! Feta omelette pastrami?' – my breakfast of choice being a feta-cheese omelette with pastrami on the side); and, best of all, it served alcohol.

In addition to the regular beer and spirits, it had a barman who'd mix up Alabama Slammers (Southern Comfort, gin and vodka, lemon juice and a dash of Grenadine, and finished off with a Galliano float) and Long Island Iced Teas (gin, vodka, white rum, tequila and Triple Sec, with a dash of Coke for colour) for us – they were ridiculously cheap and it was seldom that we didn't klap it quite heavily. It wasn't unusual to have to be carried across the road to the ship after a session in the Wanker.

§

It was easy to be in awe of the well-heeled passengers, people with apparently bottomless supplies of money, and it wasn't until I got to know a few of them a bit better that I realised that not all the 'super-wealthy' were quite as rich as they liked people to believe.

One of these was a marvellous little woman called Lila Kenneth, a French survivor of the Nazi concentration camps (if you knew where to look, you could see where she'd had the infamous tattoo lasered off). Lila, who had a shock of bright red hair and was always impeccably dressed, sailed on the *QE2* for three months every year – and she came specifically for the dancing.

Once, in Florida, I spent some time ashore with Marie, who was a friend of Lila's. (Passengers were often very kind to me when I took shore leave away from home, supplying me with all sorts of luxuries, from fabulous guest apartments to cars and maids; I would be wined and dined in fine style, and for a few short days at a time would experience what it was like not to have any money worries and to be able to indulge my every whim.)

We visited Lila at her gorgeous Palm Beach apartment. 'Will you be joining the cruise this year?' Marie asked, over cups of tea and biscuits.

Lila looked crestfallen. 'I don't think I will,' she said. 'I haven't been able to find someone to rent my apartment.'

It was then that I twigged that Lila was one of those 'ladies on a budget', and that the rental she got for her apartment was necessary for her to cover the cost of her cruise.

§

On the *QE2* I met movie stars and singers, professional athletes, high-profile businessmen, and people who were famous just for being famous. Lord Mountbatten, Lynn Redgrave, Peter Sellers, Ringo Starr, Arnold Bowie, Sir Jimmy Savile, Ben Kingsley and many of Andrew Lloyd Webber's leading ladies (Holly Lipton, who played Mary Magdalene in *Jesus Christ Superstar*; Pamela Blake (pictured), who was *Evita* on Broadway; Yvonne Elliman, another Mary Magdalene; and Sarah Brightman, who sang for us in the salon) – these were just a few of the Names that spent time cruising on the world's most famous ocean liner.

I was responsible, at one stage, for the regular bleaching of singer Bertice Reading's hair. A large, effusive African-American, Bertice loved ragging me about my country of origin. As I applied the peroxide, she would snarl at me, 'You fucking South African, you're burning me!' Then she'd smile beatifically and add, 'But I still love you.'

Petula Clark, then in her 60s, had just received her CBE from the Queen when she travelled on the *QE2*. A child movie and TV star in the UK in 1940s, she had shot to global fame in the 1960s with her hits 'Downtown' and 'Don't Sleep in the Subway'; John Lennon had once called her his favourite vocalist. Still a consummate entertainer in the 1980s, she was performing in New York in *Sunset Boulevard* (with music by Andrew Lloyd Webber), which required endless costume changes and an energetic run up and down a giant staircase.

On her passage to England, Petula was under contract to the *QE2* to perform two shows in the Grand Lounge. I watched one of them and although I thought it was stunning, I was surprised by the audience reaction, which was politely lukewarm at best.

So the following night, when she performed for mainly staff and crew in the Pig and Whistle bar, I was concerned about how she'd be received. I needn't have worried: she literally brought down the ceiling. The bar had quite a low ceiling, and as Petula segued with seamless style into a rendition of 'Downtown', the members of the audience – largely gay men – leapt to their feet, screaming their appreciation and throwing their arms up, in the process wrecking the roof.

The following night Petula appeared in the Wardroom. The audience was different here, again, and she wasn't keen to do 'Downtown' for them, perhaps thinking the vibe wasn't right. But I, who had so faithfully watched all her shows, begged her. And I can't pretend I didn't practically swoon with joy when she finally said, 'Richard, this one's for you:

Downtown,' and sang that massively famous signature song, *especially for me*.

American actor Telly 'Kojak' Savalas was another guest. Savalas, a world-class poker player, came on board with his wife for a million-dollar poker tournament that was held on the ship. I was doing his wife's hair when he popped in to the salon. Running a hand over his famous bald pate, he joked, 'I don't suppose there's anything you can do for me?'

'How about a polish?' I said, which he thought very funny.

The lollipop-loving TV cop showed a touchingly human side when a very doddery passenger, in a chair in the salon at the time, turned to him and said, 'You know, Mr Savalas, my luggage has gone missing and I don't have anything to wear. I don't suppose you could help me out?'

Who knows if she thought he might drop a couple of hundred dollars in her lap, but even if he'd had a hair to turn, he didn't. Without missing a beat, he said, with a good-natured and understanding smile, 'Let me have a rummage around in my bags. What's your cabin number? I'll drop off a few things later this evening.'

Rod Stewart and his then-wife Rachel Hunter were also passengers – twice; and both times they cruised, Rachel was pregnant. Rachel, who was 24 years younger than Rod, was Rod's second wife but the fourth woman to produce Stewart offspring – Rod's first child, a daughter, was born in 1964 to art student Susannah Boffey; he was married to Alana Hamilton from 1979 to 1984, a union that had produced two children; and he'd had a child with Kelly Emberg, who he dated from 1983 to 1990, the year he married Rachel.

A self-confessed womaniser, Rod's lifetime list of loves include model Dee Harrington, who he lived with for five years, and actress Britt Ekland, who was, he said, 'the one I should have married; she was everything I could have wanted in a woman'. Indeed, perhaps he should have: after his second divorce a reporter asked him if he still believed in matrimony and he replied, 'No. Instead of getting married again, I'm going to find a woman I don't like and just give her a house.' In the event, after Rachel left him in 1999, he got together with leggy photography student Penny Lancaster; six years later, at the age of 62, he divorced Rachel and married Penny, the mother of his seventh child, a son.

Although Rod likes to pretend he's not vain, I saw another side to him: his hair (which he called his 'barnet' – from the rhyming slang 'Barnet Fair', a reference to the well-known horse fair in the North London town of Barnet) was his pride and joy. He once told a reporter, 'I couldn't deal with it if I'd run out of barnet – imagine me with a Bobby Charlton comb-over!' Maintaining his hair's trademark spikiness was all-important but because the tap water on the ship had gone through the desalination plant and during processing had had much of its ions removed, it was very 'soft', and made Rod's hair unacceptably limp when I used it for rinsing. No problem for this multimillionaire: he just bought bottles of Evian to do the job.

Cutting Rod's hair was a unique experience: he would come to the salon (with Rachel in attendance – the pair were inseparable), sit down in the chair, splay his hands out over the top of his head, and say, 'Just cut where my hands aren't.' And Rod loved hair products – it wasn't unusual to sell him up to $300-worth of gel at a time, to keep his barnet nice and spiky.

Rumour had it that Rod had been banned from the ship for some time for breaking up a cabin; either this was a myth or by the time I was working on the *QE2* the ban had been lifted.

One very famous movie star, a married man whose sexual orientation has often been questioned in the press (a male porn star alleged he had a two-year affair with the person in question but retracted this allegation after 'discussions' with the actor's lawyers), took a fancy to one of the hairdressers, a man called Duncan who was arguably more beautiful than any of the women on the ship. Duncan was very aware of his extraordinary good looks, and flaunted these to best effect by wandering the decks clad in a risqué dress hand-made out of a black plastic bin liner. Some time later, when Duncan discovered there were also white and green bin liners to be had in the ship's stores, he upgraded his plastic dress to include these colours. (He was occasionally 'hired' by crew to be a 'kissogram girl' on the red-letter days of their colleagues, such as birthdays, and then could be seen fluttering into a public room, and covering a mortified staff member – of either gender – with kisses before flouncing out again.)

The actor, who was travelling with his 'chauffeur' whose name was given on the passenger manifest as 'John Smith', came into the salon for a trim and spotted Duncan. A few hours later I received a call from John Smith, wishing to talk to Duncan. Because stylists weren't permitted to take personal phonecalls in the salon, I took a message. 'Please join [the actor] in his cabin for drinks at 7.30pm.'

Duncan's cabin-mate, a straight hairdresser called Connell (the only heterosexual hairdresser on the staff at the time, as it happened), went into instant denial. A huge fan of the actor, Connell simply refused to believe he'd stray across the gender lines in this way. 'He's straight! I'm telling you, he's straight!' he kept muttering.

That evening, determined to prove his hero's heterosexuality, Connell hung around unhappily while Duncan readied himself for his date. Then he followed Duncan to the actor's cabin, and lurked around outside for much of the night, waiting for Duncan to re-emerge.

It was morning before Duncan stepped out, looking tired and somewhat dishevelled. Connell was furious when Duncan refused to divulge any details of his night of … was it passion? Duncan never told.

When I read in a tabloid some years later that the actor had made a pass at a business executive in the sauna of a fitness club in California, but that the man had rebuffed the actor's advances because he was chubby and 'really hairy on his back, upper arms and chest', I had to smile to myself. One of the treatments the actor had booked himself in for while he was on the *QE2* was a back wax.

6. The Theatre, Casino, Gym and Spa

There was a multitude of ways for passengers to keep themselves occupied during cruises and one of the hot favourites was gambling. But where there's big money, there's almost always also big graft, so casino staff were kept separate from the general crew: they travelled on passenger, not crew, tickets and were berthed not in the crew section but alongside the passengers. The only crew members permitted in the casino at any time were the hotel manager and the captain.

The casino staff really got up the nose of the general crew, not least because they definitely had the cushiest jobs. And the cushiest of the cushy casino jobs was that of cashier. There were two on board, and neither was permitted by law to work for longer than four hours at a stretch, so their shifts were enviably short. For we hairdressers, who battled daily through gruelling twelve-hour shifts and often worked overtime too, this was a real piss-off.

Also, because the casino – again, by law – was closed every time the ship docked, the casino staff got shore leave at every port of call. They worked only 'sea days', unlike the general crew, who often worked 'land days' too.

There was plenty more about the casino staff that irritated the crew. They wore the best uniforms, for one. They ate in one of the passenger restaurants, for another. This was a sore point for the crew, who took their meals in one of four crew messes – officers', concessionaires', women's and men's. The officers' mess had the best food – they got to eat the food not used in the 'lowest-rung' passenger restaurant, the Mauretania (the one in which the casino staff ate). The 'leftovers' from the officers' mess were handed down to the concessionaires' mess; and the leftovers from the concessionaires' mess ended up in the women's and men's messes. So those eating at the bottom of this food chain bore a culinary grudge against the casino staff.

The casino staff's cabin parties were also irksomely legendary – they earned considerably more than the rest of the crew, so were always able to roll out apparently endless supplies of booze, cigarettes and recreational drugs. And because the casino closed at 4am, that's when their parties started. It was terrifically galling to know that between 4am and 8am – when we galley slaves were getting enough shut-eye to ensure we'd get through the next onerous working day – those bastards were drinking, snorting and shagging up a storm.

As much as they considered themselves a rung above the ordinary crew by dint of having honorary passenger status, casino staff were never averse to pulling the 'I'm a crew member too' card if they needed to. So, for instance, when we were docked outside a port (the liner was too big to enter many of the ports we stopped at) and were ferried in to land in groups of about 200 at a time, the night staff always went first. Passengers went in last – and these last launches should have been the ones carrying the casino staff too (they were 'passengers', after all). But the casino staff would suddenly declare themselves, in this one instance, to be 'staff' rather than 'passengers', and push their way onto the first launches. It really rubbed us up the wrong way.

Poor social manners weren't restricted to the casino staff, however. The slot-machine aficionados in particular – many of them wobbly ladies in mail-order clothes – were known for their uncouth and sometimes aggressive behaviour. As happens in land-based casinos, in the *QE2* casino certain passengers would earmark a slot machine for their own personal use. They figured, if they fed enough coins into it for long enough, their number was bound to come up eventually.

There's only so long a human being can go, however, without needing to go; when Nature calls, you can't ignore her forever. These obsessed people would play on and on and on, crossing their legs and wriggling in increasing discomfort, unwilling to leave 'their' machines until the possibility of an embarrassing accident became a near-certainty. Then they'd dash to the men's or ladies' room as fast as their overfull bladders would allow them to, before screaming back to reclaim 'their' machines.

But sometimes they weren't quick enough, and on more than one occasion someone else slipped in, inserted a coin and watched with glee as the machine paid out by the bucketload. When the 'owner' of the machine returned, there would be heated words exchanged and actual violence wasn't unusual. More than one passenger was banned from the casino for this kind of behaviour.

The same applied – laughably – to the bingo hall. Here, little old ladies, many of them World Cruisers (as opposed to the 'day trippers', who were simply anyone not on board for the entire world cruise, and who were regarded with the most profound disdain by the World Cruisers), turned what should have been a fun pastime into a grim battle to the jackpot. And if a day tripper had the utter nerve to win it, there would be outrage all round. I had one of these sore losers in the salon the day after she'd 'lost' a jackpot to some upstart, and she was adamant: 'It's not fair!' she said grouchily. 'They should change the rules!'

These World Cruisers, who were often diamond members of the Cunard World Club (their Diamond Cunarder pins told other, lesser passengers that they'd completed either fifteen voyages or over 150 days at sea on the ship), almost always had an elevated sense of their own shipboard status. They assumed they'd get the best tables in restaurants, front-row seats at shows and preferential treatment elsewhere – and they often did; but their presumptuousness was annoying and sometimes insulting to other passengers.

The Cunard World Club held a special cocktail party in the Queen's Room for these frequent sailors – but it was truly a tick in a passenger's passport to be invited to the World Cruisers' dinner, held annually in some fabulous hotel in a city port. The best gowns and jewels would be saved for these occasions, which always meant hell in the salon, with the last appointments of the day being overtly bartered for by women who wanted their hair just so as they twinkled down the gangway and into the waiting limousines. The World Cruisers loved this occasion, when, under the envious gaze of the plebs on board, they were given the royal treatment they felt they so richly deserved.

I still have two memento menus, given as gifts to me by World Cruise Society members after these blow-out events. One, in 1994, took place in Cape Town, and the menu is printed on a collector's item Noritake plate; it includes rock lobster, smoked salmon, shiitake mushrooms, veal and fresh strawberries. The other, in 1996, from The Hong Kong Regent (and printed on a three-dimensional bamboo landscape sculpture) boasts duck breast, shark fin soup and (somewhat bizarrely) Lamb Provençale.

§

At some point during the world cruise, the crew would put on a show in the auditorium – an Art Deco-themed theatre equipped with a balcony and stage. Each department did a different skit and this was an event not to be missed: many of the staff on the liner were – like their land-based compatriots in similar occupations – enormously talented people, working menial jobs to keep body and soul together (although, on the *QE2*, with the additional benefit of travelling the world).

Although the crew show was specifically *not* for passengers – it was put on by the crew for the crew – it wasn't unusual for favoured passengers to be surreptitiously slipped its date and time. On a liner like the *QE2*, nobody would 'stop' a passenger from doing more or less whatever they wanted, so if a passenger turned up to watch the crew's performance, they were of course admitted. (More than once, a passenger who'd snuck in to watch the show told me that they thought it was of a better standard than the 'official' entertainment put on in the public rooms!)

So, because passengers did often see the crew show, the captain gave some very strict guidelines about what was and wasn't allowed on stage. No nudity was a given. No men in drag were permitted. No live sex may seem to be stating the obvious, but I'm not exaggerating when I say it wasn't entirely beyond some crew members to have given a no-holds-barred display if they got the chance.

So when Sandra, a superbly well-endowed hairdresser, said she wanted to do Chris de Burgh's 'Patricia the Stripper' with Connell (the straight male hairdresser) playing 'the judge', the captain was adamant: nipple caps would be worn, as would a G-string. Sandra, pouting a little, agreed.

That year's show went off wonderfully as usual – Sandra was a hit, of course – and when it was over, the performers lined up on the stage and waited for the captain to come and congratulate them and say a few parting words to the audience, as he did every year.

Sandra, in the meantime, had changed out of her stripper's costume and into a boob-tube dress – and was braless underneath it. In the spirit of the moment, Connell hoisted her onto his shoulders, elevating her above everyone else. Then, as the captain walked up the stage steps, the person standing behind Sandra yanked down her dress, exposing her ample assets for the entire audience to see.

This awesome sight was greeted, as they say in the song, 'to tremendous applause' and the crowd really was 'yelling out for more'. The captain, who'd never before received such an enthusiastic response to his closing address, looked suitably gracious and humble while he thanked the audience – not realising for one minute that it wasn't his inspirational words that were causing the cat-calls and wolf-whistles, but Sandra, standing behind him with her tits out.

Sandra, whose joie de vivre was near-legendary, performed another costume fantasy for a captive audience. In the late 1980s there was a lot of dissent in the ranks of the National Union of Seamen, and strike actions in Southampton became the order of the day. At one point all of the *QE2* staff joined in a mass-action march to the Cunard offices, an event that was widely televised in the UK.

It happened to be the day on which Sandra also got married, to a Wardroom bartender with whom she'd been in a relationship for several years. Sandra had no problem whatsoever in combining these two wholly disparate occasions, and turned up, in full frilly white wedding dress, her new husband held tightly by the hand, to join her colleagues in the march.

I've seldom got such a kick as I did that evening, watching the BBC news. There was Sandra, being interviewed by a serious journalist, standing on the gangway of the *QE2*, and giving her studied opinion on the strike – in full bridal regalia.

§

Although Steiner had been operating hair and beauty salons on the *QE2* from 1968, and salons and spas on a number of other cruise ships from 1987, it wasn't until 1994 that the *QE2* got its Steiner spa. Then, the company employed a team of architects to create a custom spa for the liner, which became the first ship afloat to offer a fully functioning thalassotherapy pool and related treatments, including mud baths, underwater showers, hydromassage, aromatherapy, and seaweed, mud and algae wraps, an inhalation chamber (to help clear the respiratory tract), and all the fittings and fripperies necessary for the steaming, pummelling, freezing, hosing-down and otherwise aqua-treating of our discerning passengers.

The spa was situated below water level, on 6 Deck. The thalassotherapy pool with its multi-levelled jets was filled directly from the sea, and for this reason it was fitted with sensors that could tell the bridge – after hours, when no staff was in the spa itself to keep an eye on things – if the water level was rising. Obviously, if the pool's inlet valves opened and for some reason didn't close, flooding became a real danger, so the warning light up on the bridge was checked regularly through the night.

Around this time a new general manager was appointed by Steiner. A harridan called Vicky, she quickly made herself exceedingly unpopular. She was entirely devoid of people skills, and simply couldn't bring herself to get things done without putting someone's back up. She was thoroughly disliked by everyone who worked under her, and most of us couldn't wait for the day when this ridiculous woman, who tarted around in sky-high heels making everyone's life a misery, got her come-uppance.

Vicky considered herself far too good to associate with mere crew, and hung around with the officers. Sometimes she hung around with them horizontally.

One red-letter night, Vicky took one of her lovers (a married man, as it happened) down to the spa. She had the keys and she had the power – why not flash both around a bit and impress her beau with a bit of a romp in the hot bath?

Alas for Vicky, she'd forgotten that the sensors in the thalassotherapy pool were activated at night, so that the crew on the bridge could keep a weather eye on the water levels. So as soon as Vicky and her lover lowered themselves into the water, the level rose and – eureka! – up on the bridge, a red warning light flashed on.

It took the duty officer long enough to get down to 6 Deck that by the time he arrived at the spa, Vicky and her married lover were giving it loads. Bust!

And of course, the reality of living in a floating village is that nothing stays secret for long. For some time afterwards, when Vicky tried to order people around, there would be someone quick to say, 'Keeping an eye on the water levels there, Vicky?'

The spa also had a steam room, which was open to passengers from 6am to 9pm. It was originally unsupervised but this changed when the captain went down for a quick sauna before his shift started and was propositioned not once, not twice, but three times by horny men with tented towels. Declaring himself unwilling to be in charge of a liner with the first and only floating bath house in the world, he put a staff member on duty during the hours the steam room was open.

§

When Steiner took over the *QE2*'s spa, the company also took responsibility for the gym – Steiner had moved from simple hairdressing to an overall philosophy that focused on beauty and wellbeing. As part of this revamped thinking, Steiner expected *all* its employees, regardless of their occupation within the group, to reflect not only beauty but health and fitness too.

For hairstylists who were used to working hard and playing harder, this was a true body-shock. And when Steiner introduced what it called 'The Essential Workout' for its personnel, we thought we'd died and gone straight to hell. This 20-minute workout, which focused on aerobics and light weight-training, was required to be completed by all Steiner staff six times a week – three times on Steiner's time and (outrageously) three times in our own time. And there was no getting out of it: the gym bunnies kept detailed records of who had completed the workout and when.

(An incentive was that Steiner staff were permitted to wear the official gym togs as part of this health drive, which we quite fancied: it was pretty cool striding out on the deck in the mornings in those sexy little shorts and trainers, and the designer shell suit that was part of the package wasn't too shabby either.)

QUEEN ELIZABETH 2 Photographed on board 1994

Still, the 'own time' sessions were particularly infuriating – we worked twelve-hour days, so finding time to jump around wasn't easy. But, faced with the choice of getting fit or getting fired, we stylists decided to get together in the gym

142

three times a week, either at 6 in the morning before work or at 10 in the evening after, and do it together.

The first few sessions were disastrous. We were hairdressers, not health fanatics, and the lack of coordination (not to mention enthusiasm) was laughable. People windmilled their arms, fell off step machines, dropped dumb-bells on their toes, passed out breathless or fell down giggling. Fingers were cruelly pointed at those who had no rhythm; smokers wished they weren't; drinkers (usually nursing nasty hangovers) swore they'd never touch another drop.

But, a month later, with 24 Essential Workouts under our belts, we noticed something remarkable: we had, without intending to (or even vaguely hoping we could), become a fairly well-oiled machine. Everyone had grown accustomed to the routine and most of us had actually become quite good at it.

And four months after that, many of us had officially become gym bunnies! Not only were we passionate about our six-times-weekly workouts, some of us had begun doing additional exercise on our own. Four of us – me included – would take every possible opportunity at port stops to get into our sweats and running shoes and go jogging.

It was around this time that actor/singer/dancer/choreographer Gregory Hines (probably most famous for his tap dancing, he had appeared in movies like *The Cotton Club* and *White Nights* in which he co-starred with ballet supremo Mikhail Baryshnikov) came on board with his second wife, theatrical producer Pamela Koslow. Hines – a health nut who, with sad irony, died of liver cancer in 2003 – was blown away by our dedication to fitness, and one morning in New York, when the four of us were preparing for our morning jog, asked where we'd be going. We described our routine to him – a ten-kilometre run through Central Park, and then a leisurely breakfast at the Great American Health Bar on West 57th Street.

'I'll meet you there,' Hines said.

Yeah, right, we thought, and set off for our run. At the Great American Health Bar we had to queue for seats, as usual, and we were just getting the smoothies we'd ordered when… in walked Gregory and his wife.

This wonderfully congenial man sat down and joined us for breakfast, as he'd promised.

And we never had to queue for seats at the Great American Health Bar again!

§

It's probably worth mentioning that the *QE2* big-screen cinema, once the largest at sea, regularly showed both the 1972 blockbuster 'disaster movie' *The Poseidon Adventure*, starring Gene Hackman, in which an ocean liner capsizes at sea and a group of passengers struggle to survive and escape (it's tagline: 'Hell. Upside Down'); and the 1997 Oscar 'king of the world', *Titanic*, with Kate Winslet and Leonardo Di Caprio, about the sinking of the RMS *Titanic* in 1912. Strange but true.

7. Public Rooms – Restaurants, Bars and Lounges

'What time is the midnight buffet?'

I was asked so many stupid questions by passengers that it would take another book to list them all but this was my favourite. It was very hard not to pull a *Mad* magazine 'snappy answers to stupid questions' on these gormless individuals but as a crew member of one of the most illustrious liners on the high seas, alas, I couldn't. 'At midnight, sir,' I would say, with a guileless smile.

(Another choice stupid question came from passengers who would ask, standing outside the lift at G stairway, 'Does this elevator go to A stairway?' It took the intelligence of a geranium to work out that the ship's stairways were arranged horizontally, not vertically. Where the hell did they think they were, in Willy Wonka's Chocolate Factory?

(Of course we got our own back on these silly people. My own preferred line was to warn irritating passengers about the 'bump' as we crossed the equator, and have a wicked little chuckle to myself when they not only took me seriously but warned their fellow passengers about it too.)

The midnight buffet was the sixth and last meal served each day. Aside from the à la carte menus available in all four of the restaurants during normal 'working' hours, there were breakfast, lunch and the midnight buffets; and after hours round-the-clock room service was available for those who might still not have eaten enough.

So passengers leaving the bar after one too many or coming out of a show late at night could hit the buffet for a last gastric blow-out, including full hot and cold spreads and any number of extras that could be ordered on the side.

And then there were also the 'gala' buffets, featuring chocolates from around the world, for instance, or centring on a particular theme (ice, say, or Halloween); sculptures in butter and fruit were favourites; and the gorgeously decorated cakes and marzipan animals were so admired that sometimes the buffet was opened half an hour early so passengers could come and take photographs.

(So, okay, I suppose the answer to the 'What time is the midnight buffet?' question could very well have been '11.30'.)

The *QE2*'s laundry (about which more later), a marvel of organisation and workmanship, occasionally received complaints from passengers who had got back garments that had apparently 'shrunk' in the wash. Believe me: they hadn't.

And it wasn't unusual to overhear passengers, cramming just one more melt-in-the-mouth croissant or spectacularly iced petit-four into their cakehole, remark on how the 'sea air' had done weird things to their clothes as a result of which they didn't fit any more.

There were also a series of cocktail parties for passengers in the various public rooms. The first two nights were open to all on board – these were the 'captain's cocktails', when all passengers were invited to meet (and be photographed with, if they wished) the captain. On subsequent nights the doctor might host a cocktail party, then the hotel manager, then the first officer – these were all by invitation only and invites were highly sought-after.

The Wardroom Reception, usually held on the last night, was the cherry on top of these social gatherings, and for a passenger to crack the nod to one of these was considered a privilege indeed.

The high-rolling passengers held their own 'private' cocktail parties too. Sometimes they'd host these in their penthouse suites; sometimes a public room was hired for the evening and closed to the non-invited. The passenger holding the party footed the bill, but the party was, obviously, catered, organised, managed and staffed by the QE2. The best gowns and jewels, bibs and tuckers were rolled out for these, and it was always entertaining to see how the super-wealthy (or those pretending to be) tried to outdo each other – and how invites to these private do's became social currency.

Not receiving an 'in' to a certain private cocktail party could be such a snub that the uninvited might spend the rest of the cruise skulking around in their cabins, too embarrassed to show their faces.

§

For all the shenanigans that went on behind the scenes, the *QE2* staff were remarkably civil to and respectful of their clients – even the difficult ones.

There were, of course, the occasional cockups in the kitchen – once, the chef sliced off the tip of his finger while making pea-and-ham soup and never located the missing bit, which quite likely ended up in the stomach of an oblivious diner – but I think it's fair to say that the *QE2* crew took out their frustrations far less frequently on their difficult passengers than what's reported from the hotel industry around the world.

But even if revenge wasn't common, when it happened, it was sweet. The use of a judicious squirt of eye drops (Optrex was in abundant supply on the boat) in a cup of tea of coffee, after a perfectly good plate of food ordered and sent back for no good reason - and sometimes sent back again for, again, no good reason - wasn't unknown. (It's been said that the use of eye drops in restaurant beverages to cause diarrhoea is an urban myth; I can tell you it's not.)

Interestingly, this drizzling-shits treatment wasn't necessarily to punish the whingeing diner; it was just to get him or her out of the waiters' hair: an unreasonably fussy passenger who'd got a side order of Optrex with their post-prandial digestif usually felt unwell enough not to darken the restaurant door for at least a few days.

We Steiner managers occasionally ate in the Mauretania restaurant along with the passengers. The waiters who were assigned to our tables (there was no self-service) weren't thrilled with the arrangement as, obviously, it was unlikely they were going to get any tips from us.

We got our own back on them for their desultory and sometimes downright petulant service by ordering the two things waiters hated most to make: Horlicks, which required heating milk and some vigorous and time-wasting stirring; and tea, the process for which (heating the teapot, setting the tray, organising milk and sugar, etc) was similarly considered a hassle.

The waiters, in their turn, punished us for this. A little bit of hashish lightly toasted in a burner and thoroughly stirred into a mug of Horlicks could cause merry havoc for the drinker and much hilarity for the put-upon waiters. As for the tea order, the waiter taking it would wilfully misunderstand and bring, instead of hot Ceylon tea, a glass of potently alcoholic Long Island Iced Tea. Rather than lose face by sending it back, the staff member would often drink it – and then have to struggle, half-pissed, through their afternoon shift.

A regular party that left crew pie-eyed and stumbling through the day was the monthly German breakfast, held below decks in the cold-storage rooms. These affairs, hosted by the German galley staff and to which German passengers were invited, were all about the national flag, oompah music, sauerkraut, bratwurst, dumplings, pumpernickel, kirschtorte, strudel … and, of course, endless quantities of schnapps and Jegermeister.

The breakfast kicked off at 10am, and entry was gained only after an invitee had agreed to drink a 'Toxic Sludge' – a jelly-shot made with clear spirit. From there, things deteriorated beautifully, and the event went on for as long as there were people standing.

For the intoxicated passengers, who could escape to their cabins and sleep off their excesses, the after-shocks of the German breakfast weren't a problem; for the staff, who had to get through a working afternoon, they weren't always worth the fun.

Marc – the assistant restaurant manager who, when I first joined the ship, taught me all I needed to know about how to conduct sexual conquests without having to deal with consequences – had a particularly hard time doing his job once, after he and I took some shore leave in Tenerife.

We'd got ashore at about 8am and ordered a jug of sangria to go with our breakfast – when in tropical climes, after all, why not do as the natives do? It was so fruity and delicious that we klapped it quickly, and ordered another. And, as these things go, pretty soon had to order another. And another.

By midday we were dizzy with drink and disporting ourselves with great delight on the beach. Suddenly, Marc clapped his hand to his forehead. 'Jesus!' he said. 'I'm on duty this afternoon!'

One of Marc's learned skills was flambéing – it was a feature in the Queen's Grill restaurant (one of the poshest on board) for diners to be able to order crêpes Suzettes for dessert, which would be prepared at the table. It was no easy to task to deal with delicate batter, open flames and highly flammable alcohol on a wheeled trolley when the ship was riding out a gale, but Marc had aced this particular talent and always accomplished it with flair and decorum.

Unless, that is, he had several pitchers of sangria sloshing about inside him.

After very nearly setting himself alight that lunchtime, to the great alarm of his guests, Marc was excused from duties on grounds of 'ill health'.

§

One guest who loved a good party was British actress-comedienne Su Pollard, probably most famous for her role in the BBC television series *Hi De Hi!*, which notched almost sixty episodes and ran until 1988. In her 40s during the time she cruised on the *QE2*, her very individual sense of style already had her labelled as one of the wackiest dressers in the UK. Now in her 60s and still performing, she hasn't lost any of her zest for the outrageous. In an April 2009 interview with the *Mail Online*, she pointedly said, 'There are a lot of grey people out there in the world – but I'm not one of them.'

Indeed not! Her favourite outfit when she was 8 years old was reportedly a yellow polka-dot-on-blue smock dress with yellow tights and black patent-leather shoes. Although her mother tried to coax her into something 'less gregarious', she stuck to her sartorial guns and wore the outfit regularly until she was 12 and '"front bumps" in the chest area began to emerge and the buttons pinged off'. At school she wore the uniform cape around her neck like Supergirl (for which she regularly got detention). In her 20s one of her favourite pieces was a pink, green, yellow and purple striped dress so short 'I could have been a porn star'. Today she's still regularly seen wearing eyebrow-raisingly short miniskirts; and why shouldn't she, she asks: 'I've been told that I have the legs of a 25-year-old.'

Su and I became good friends and when I went ashore with her in the UK it was always a bit of a thrill – she was a Name and recognised everywhere she went, and I can't pretend I didn't enjoy basking in her limelight.

This was shortly after Barbra Streisand's love affair with her hairdresser, the much-married (and equally much divorced) Jon Peters, was in the news. Peters, a flamboyant but not terribly likeable character, used his contact with Barbra to get into Hollywood and became a producer of movies such as *A Star is Born* (with Barbra in the lead role), *Batman* (with Jack Nicholson as The Joker) and *Superman Returns*; Peters was reportedly the model for the womanising hairdresser played by Warren Beatty in the 1975 hit movie *Shampoo*.

So it was against this background that Su and I went to the Lido one evening. Although I wasn't all that keen, Su loved to dance, and she spent the evening pestering me to join her on the floor. Finally, nearing midnight and unable to find any more excuses not to, I took her hand and led her out onto the dance floor. There, Su pretended to swoon into my arms and declared, 'Ooh! I feel just like Barbra, dancin' with me 'airdresser!'

The Lido, which was the ship's casual eatery and where buffets were served, had a clear Perspex dance floor underlit with coloured lights, so was a perfect venue for the fashion shows that were held on the first night of every trans-Atlantic crossing. These were really just an excuse to advertise the designer-wear available in the onboard boutiques – every big name in the business was represented, from Gucci and Ralph Lauren to Lacoste and Armani, and there was always a range of tip-top tartans.

The fashion shows would be kicked off, literally, by the Peter Gordino dancers, who took to the floor at midnight on the dot. Once they'd finished their routine, the fashion parade itself would start.

The models for these shows were the shop assistants and the Steiner stylists, and for this pleasure we would each be given a few perfume testers from the top perfumeries in the world (I still have a box of them!). We each had four outfit changes, and each series of outfits would be presented in a carefully choreographed scenario according to its purpose – for the coats, for instance, the Lido's smoke machine was dragged into use, and we 'models' would slink out onto the runway in Burberry and Aquascutum, moving through the 'fog' as if we were in London on a misty day.

At one of these fashion shows I was required to dress in full tartan, down to kilt and sporran (the pouch that hangs in the front), and dance the Gay Gordons with a Peter Gordino dancer as my partner. This is an old-fashioned dance, with each couple dancing the same steps, usually around the room – or, in our case, across the Lido dance floor. There's a bit of spinning and some fairly energetic polka-type steps involved, and we'd spent some time practising it to make sure we'd got it perfect.

I was waiting my turn to appear, going through the dance steps in my head, when a dresser suddenly appeared at my side. 'Are you wearing underpants?' she asked.

'Of course!' I said. Not only was the kilt scratchy, but I had no intention of exposing my dangly bits to the *QE2*'s passengers should my kilt fly up during the more lively parts of the dance.

'Take them off,' she snapped.

'You've got to be kidding!' I said.

'We're advertising the real deal here,' she said. 'Real Scotsmen don't wear underwear. Take them off.'

I opened my mouth to argue but just then I heard the compère call my item. 'Fuck,' I muttered under my breath, and, under the beady eye of the dresser, I whipped off my jockies.

I was nervous as my partner and I headed into our first whirl but quickly realised that the sporran serves the useful purpose of keeping the kilt down, and that the system of pins and buckles that secure the kilt also keep it quite close to the body. So I relaxed, and the dancer and I completed our Gay Gordons in fine style.

Right up until the last step.

The dance ended with a flourish at the audience side of the dance floor, and as we did our last whirl and came to a stop, my feet slid out from under me. Still moving forward as a result of the momentum of the dance, I could do nothing but shriek helplessly as I skidded off the dance floor, taking my partner with me. We both ended up under a table – me with my kilt right up over my head.

As I got unsteadily to my feet amidst cheers and catcalls, the passenger sitting at the table we'd ended up under said admiringly, 'So, you *are* a real Scotsman!' (I did wonder, briefly, if this overexposure would help sales or hinder them.)

Steiner occasionally took over the Lido to do what we called 'hair-raising' parties, with the same objective as the fashion shows – to advertise our products and services. These shows would also start at midnight and were a bit more vibey than the fashion shows, with more emphasis on having fun. We'd dress up all in white and offset this clean look with wild makeup and brightly coloured wigs, and during the hair-raising we'd give away vouchers and a selection of products before mingling and partying with the passengers.

One year we decided to start the hair-raising with a rendition of Michael Jackson's 'Thriller'. This fourteen-minute-long 'best music video ever' had wowed the world, with US music television station MTV having to play it twice an hour to keep up with demand. We sent out invitations to the passengers with what we thought was a cleverly worded little bit of verse:

> *We give you from this Cunard liner*
> *Ghosts and ghouls and things from Steiner.*
> *Come and see our midnight show*
> *From a group you'll love to know.*
> *Steiners know just what to do*

When you're feeling down and blue.
So come along to be refreshed
And put our stylists to the test.
From hair and beauty to footcare too,
Every service just for you.
Come let's spoil you before you go
And relax at Steiner from top to toe.

Our take on the ghoulish dance sequence proved such a hit that *Good Morning America*, the US's breakfast television news and talk show, decided they wanted to film us.

We spent some hectic days fine-tuning our performance, making sure that our costumes and makeup were perfect and our dance steps flawless. When the big day arrived we were more than ready.

Sadly, the smoke machine wasn't. For some reason, it malfunctioned, and instead of sending out eerie wisps, it pumped out great clouds. We battled our way through our sequence, barely able to see each other through the haze, and when it was over the producer rolled his eyes, switched off the cameras and stalked away, unimpressed. So we didn't get our fourteen minutes of fame.

But not all the promo parties were glitz and glamour. One of them, in later years, was initiated to illustrate all the wonderful 'health' (ie, slimming) products Steiner had to offer. One of these was 'ionothermy inch-loss' therapy, a so-called cellulite-fighting treatment which required, basically, that clients subject themselves to a series of fat-jarring electrical shocks; and the other was some kind of sit-and-sweat therapy, where up to a cupful of perspiration could be scooped off a customer in a single session (yeuch).

But it wasn't the inherent untruths in these demos that freaked out those among us unlucky enough to be 'nominated' (as if we had a choice) to act as models. It was that we were required to be near-naked: after all, the treatments being demonstrated required clients to divest themselves of all clothing. And, given that actual nudity wasn't allowed, our dignity was further impaired by our being forced to wear paper knickers for the duration of these very public sessions, which were attended by, sometimes, upwards of 300 people. I sometimes still wake up in cold sweats in the small hours, thinking of this.

The crew often pushed the envelope when it came to regulations, and one time we did this, we inadvertently got someone into trouble. It was the birthday of one of the shop managers, and we decided, as a special treat, to do something different for the final walk-on in that evening's fashion show. Although we were specifically forbidden to dress in drag, we thought this one time we could bend the rules, and we really went to town. All the boys got dressed up in women's clothes and we raided the makeup drawers and wig cupboards. I wore a long green skirt with a lace top and a curly blonde wig that went fabulously with the moustache I had at the time.

The show went off wonderfully but the shop manager, who was held responsible for the gaggle of drag queens who sashayed out for the finale, was hauled up before the captain and given a severe bollocking and a written warning. It wasn't the birthday present we'd envisaged for him.

§

The public areas of the ship were no place to be during heavy weather. When the captain made his announcement that rough seas were on the horizon, small white bags would begin appearing in all the public rooms and corridors. These were barf bags, and the hope was that nauseated passengers would use them – although this didn't always happen. So these occasions came to be known as 'pavement pizza days', when green-gilled passengers would deposit little piles of multicoloured puke everywhere. The Filipinos whose thankless job it was to clean up these leavings would fling a white powder over them top of them and wait for them to dry out before vacuuming them up.

For those who suffer it, sea-sickness is truly ghastly. It's caused, apparently, by visual confusion, when the supposedly fixed lines of nearby objects move with the motion of the ship. But victims really couldn't give a monkey's what causes it: they just want it to stop. There's a famous Isaac Azimov quote in which a ship's steward cheerfully informs an ill passenger that nobody has ever died of seasickness, and the passenger replies, 'Please! It's only the hope of dying that's keeping me alive!'

There were, of course, many ways sea-sickness could be circumvented. Passengers who suffered from the malady could choose between a pill and an injection, both of which would stop the nausea, but both of which would also cause debilitating tiredness, with the result that they often spent several days of the cruise conked out in their cabins.

Then the ship's pharmacy started selling skin patches which, when plastered behind the ear, cured nausea caused by motion, with the added benefit of not having unconsciousness as a side effect. The passengers, who understandably didn't want to spend several expensive days at sea fast asleep, particularly on the shorter trans-Atlantic crossings, loved them.

But these patches did have some rather curious side effects. The first we knew of them was when Helga, an admin clerk in the purser's office, had to deal with a very anxious passenger, who reeled up to her and demanded that she call a taxi for him. Immediately.

Helga smiled politely. 'I'm afraid I can't do that, sir,' she said. 'We're in the middle of the Atlantic Ocean.'

'Don't be ridiculous, woman,' the passenger railed. 'I'm due on the *QE2* in a few hours. If I don't get a ride there this minute, I'll miss the boat.'

'You are already on the *QE2*, sir,' Helga said.

The poor man became so fired up with indignation that Helga, afraid for his mental health and her safety, surreptitiously called down to the infirmary and asked a doctor to come and help her. When the doctor – who presumably knew what havoc the anti-nausea patches could play with people's minds – arrived in the purser's office, he instructed the anxious man to sit down, then he said, clearly and quietly, 'Sir: remove the patch from behind your ear.'

Because the patches didn't have this mildly hallucinatory effect on too many people, and the passengers liked them because they didn't cause overwhelming sleepiness, the pharmacy continued to supply them to those who wanted them. But we staff quickly learnt to recognise patched-up clients who were on their own missions, and if someone reeled past with a glassy look in their eyes, we'd hum that weird 'Twilight Zone' music – 'doo-doo, doo-doo, doo-doo' – and grin at each other.

(Incidentally, tetrahydrocannabinol or THC, the active chemical in marijuana, is a known anti-nausea remedy. Which explains quite a lot, at least where the staff were concerned.)

Astonishingly, even inclement weather didn't keep some passengers from their salon appointments. Even though when the seas were rough passengers were advised to stay in their cabins, it wasn't unusual, when we were bobbing around like corks, battling to keep bottles, cans, hairdryers, brushes and sundry other equipment from flying off surfaces, for some little old lady to come clawing her way in, irritable and exhausted from having fought the bucking motions of the ship all the way to the salon. And these were always the ones who wanted to look like Grace Kelly – which required, of course, the full hands-on treatment: shampoo, blowdry (they never wanted rollers, for some reason) and a finishing-off with a curling iron.

Working with super-hot equipment on super-short and often super-fine hair in conditions like these was super-dangerous, but our patrons didn't care. 'Don't burn me,' would be the snappy injunction, while we stylists would stand, braced as well as we could behind our querulous clients, and the odd manicure girl went whipping past us at high speed from one side of the salon to the other, holding for dear life onto her wheelie-trolley.

§

There were four crew-only bars on board the ship: Castaways (unofficially, the 'gay bar'), the Pig and Whistle (mainly the haunt of the engineers and deck hands), the Fo'c's'le Club (which was members-only) and The Wardroom (for the officers). Castaways opened at 11pm and officially closed at 3am, whereafter those in the know could obtain drinks (and drugs) through a side hatch.

As a manager, I had membership in all the crew bars and also all the passenger bars, and was expected to mix and mingle at the numerous cocktail parties. The bar was open for these events, and the champagne-and-orange-juice coolers served to passengers on their arrival were free of charge too; and, if all the passengers didn't know that, the crew certainly did, and we took full advantage.

Getting through those cocktail parties wasn't always easy and I often smoothed the way with my tipple of choice at the time, Bacardi and Coke: one tot of Coke to about five measures of Bacardi was how I liked it.

Sometimes I'd forget that this was my standing order with the barman, and I'd be chatting to a well-heeled passenger or, sometimes, the captain, when my first drink of the evening would be brought to me by a waiter. 'Thanks,' I'd say, whipping it off the tray and taking a big swig. The alcohol would hit my palate like a hammer, bringing stinging tears to my eyes and rendering me splutteringly incapable of speech for several minutes.

Another 'little helper' for getting through those cocktail parties in those drug-fuelled 1980s was what I called 'the camel': before I left my cabin, all gussied up for the evening, I'd take a small bite of hashish. It would take about an hour to start kicking in, by which time the party was usually in full swing, and then I'd really enjoy myself.

Being a big drinker was considered a mark of achievement among the crew. Myself and three other staff members – a photographer, an Elizabeth Arden rep whom we called 'Elizabeth Hard-on', and a band member called Colin who, for his huge ears, soon became known as 'The FA Cup' –

began a club we called 'Alcoholics Synonymous', or AS, and we even went so far as to have badges made.

To earn one of these and membership of the club, a staff member had to fall over drunk in one of the public rooms. Stumbling and tripping didn't count – it was required that you had to actually fall over and not be able to get up again. Believe it or not, membership of AS was highly sought-after!

One of the 'activities' that often took place after hours in Castaways was 'bin diving' – which was exactly what it sounds like. By then most of us would be three sheets to the wind, and it seemed to us a jolly good idea to choose an ordinary black bin (into which, during the course of the evening, would have been deposited any number of bottles, glasses and other potentially dangerous debris) and, without bothering to empty it first, place it at one end of the room.

The challenge then was to take a short run-up and launch yourself long-jump style from the other end of the room, the objective being to land head-first in the bin. The winner was the person who managed the longest jump. The fact that I can't remember any injuries from this game probably says more about my state of mind when we played it than any actual wounds that resulted.

§

I once did a stint as a 'bar cashier', during an unusual six-month period in 1989 when the *QE2* was moored in Tokyo and Osaka under private charter. The Japanese were fascinated with the ship, and this was the second time it had been permanently moored in that country, serving as a floating hotel.

The cruise staff were replaced by Japanese hostesses, whom I quickly learnt to loathe: these ridiculously pretty women were serious competition to the gay contingent on board, and it was terribly irksome to watch while a desirable man who was beginning to show encouraging signs of turning suddenly reverted to total heterosexuality. Not only that, but these gorgeous little Eastern dolls managed, before our disbelieving eyes, to apparently turn more than one gay man straight!

Because, while at anchor in Japan, Steiner wasn't allowed to operate as a hair salon (for reasons to do with local employment laws), the twenty Steiner crew kept on board were reassigned as 'bar cashiers'. We were all given lists of Japanese words to learn – 'o-hayou gozaimasu' (good morning), 'sayounara' (goodbye), 'doumo arigatou gozaimasu' (thank you very much), 'o-sake' (alcohol), 'rakai desu ne' (expensive, isn't it?) – and provided with new uniforms, which included a very natty black jersey emblazoned with the *QE2* logo.

Being a bar cashier wasn't a sinecure – with the ship's nine public bars, lounges and restaurants having changed systems for this period from chits (where passengers signed for drinks, which were then put onto their bill to be presented at the end of the voyage) to cash, it was necessary to keep a very sharp eye on where the money went.

Graft, theft and general corruption is rife in the hospitality trade, and it's particularly virulent where alcohol is involved. From simple scams like watering down spirits to more complicated ones involving pocketing cash, the number of ways a company can be ripped off by its employers is legion. During our briefing prior to the Tokyo/Osaka mooring, we were made aware of this by an officer who told us, 'We know we're not going to be able to *stop* the stealing. All we want to do, really, is make sure that when the bar staff return to England after this stint, they buy Minis, not Rolls Royces.'

He was right. In spite of a complex and fairly rigorous system of checks and controls, we weren't able to entirely prevent theft. Most interesting for me, however, was the fact that, although I kept my eyes scanned and my ears pricked, I never once saw anything untoward; however the scammers went about their business, they did so with such sly discretion that they were never caught.

Coincidentally, while my co-author and I were writing this book, we met a man who had served on the *QE2* during this mooring and who had, in fact, run one of these scams. Wicked Mick told us, with some glee, about how he had turned the cash system to his advantage.

'There was a permanent band on the ship at the time, and I was friendly with quite a few of the guys in it. One of the perks of their job was that they didn't have to pay cash for their drinks – they could just sign a chit, and at the end of the month they were charged only 10% of the total bill.

'Now, a number of these guys were recovering alcoholics and never touched anything stronger than Coke. I had a quiet word with six or seven of them – telling them individually not to say a word to anyone about what I was suggesting, of course.

'My scam was simple but brilliantly effective. When a legitimate guest ordered a drink from the bar, I would present the bill immediately and the guest would pay cash. These weren't piffling amounts – the drinks were very expensive; a double whisky, which was very popular, cost $25.

'If it was a particularly juicy bill, say, over $100, I would discreetly pocket the cash. Then I would reprint the bill and take it to one of the band members. The band member would then sign for it and I would immediately give him half of the cash, which I had ready in a small envelope.

'This way, the bill went through the system as a band member's expense, not an over-the-counter cash transaction. I pocketed 50% of it; and the band member, after he'd paid 'his' 10% of the accumulated bills at the end of the month, ended up with 40% of the total in cash.

'If the purser became suspicious when processing these month-end bills for alcohol for men who were, after all, known to be teetotallers, the cover story was that the Japanese mooring was so stressful that it had turned them back to drink!'

By the end of his two-month stint in Japan, Wicked Mick had accumulated $20 000 in under-the-counter cash. But his wasn't the biggest haul. 'I learned later,' he told us, 'that one of the guys who stayed for the whole six months made so much money out of his scam that he bought a house for cash when he got back to England.'

Wicked Mick's wasn't the only scam, and he admits that, although he shared a cabin with three other public room stewards who were all running scams, none of them ever shared the details with the others – the particulars of the various scams were closely and jealously guarded, so it's not surprising that I was never able to run any of them to ground.

I was aware, of course, of the petty theft, and not least because I benefited from it. I was forever being issued with 'free' drinks, cigarettes, phone cards and the like. I knew that cash for these items didn't go into the system, for the simple reason that I never paid for them; yet, somehow, at the end of the day, the stock and takings totals always tallied.

As a job, being a bar cashier didn't have much going for it (aside from relatively better pay and perks). Not only did the people we worked with know that we were there to keep an eye on them and, if possible, catch them out, but on slow days it could be deathly boring. And when on duty we were required to be alert at all times, so doing crossword puzzles or reading the newspaper to pass the time wasn't allowed. Instead, we Steiner staff began a list of synonyms for homosexuals, which I kept in my pocket.

Several times a day, someone would rush in and whisper urgently in my ear. Anyone watching might have thought that

I was receiving an important dispatch from the captain; in fact, I was just getting yet another rude word to add to my inventory. It's a measure, perhaps, of how bored we sometimes were that the list reached 74 by the time we lost interest in it; among the expected offerings of 'fairy', 'queer', 'queen', 'moffie', 'poo-jabber' and 'fag' were 'Hershey highwayman', 'shirt-lifter', 'poephol pirate', 'butthole bandit', 'nancy-boy', 'rear gunner' and that old favourite 'friend of Dorothy'.

The origins of this last phrase, incidentally, are attributed variously to the Dorothy played by gay icon Judy Garland in the movie *The Wizard of Oz*, who was accepting of those who were different, including the gentle lion who declares, 'I'm afraid there's no denying/ I'm just a dandy lion'; and celebrated New York humorist and writer Dorothy Parker, whose close circle of friends and colleagues included gay men at a time when it was illegal to engage in homosexual acts.

There's a story (which may be apocryphal) that in the 1980s the United States' Naval Investigative Service, unaware of this euphemism for being gay, launched a massive hunt for a woman named Dorothy whom they thought to be at the centre of a ring of homosexual military personnel!

Queen Elizabeth 2

During this permanent mooring I was occasionally commandeered to help with the embarkations – of which we regularly did two every day. A group of Japanese (sometimes as few as 300 but often over a thousand) would come on board for lunch, see a show, and then disembark; the second embarkation would come on board for dinner, see a show and sleep over before disembarking the next day.

The stereotyping of Japanese as enthusiastic happy-snappers held true: embarking clients (mostly women – they partied while their businessman-husbands, similarly proving the truth of that other Japanese stereotype, worked) were invited to have their photographs taken with either a Beefeater or a Highland Guard, and I often dressed up in a kilt (with underpants!), slung a set of bagpipes over my shoulder, and posed with an endless stream of giggling Japanese women, all of them immaculately dressed in traditional kimonos and flawlessly made up.

We did, from time to time, return to our primary function as hairdressers – when the ship sailed out of port for three- or four-day cruises around the Indian Ocean. On one of these occasions I had a Japanese client with fine hair cut in a very short bob who presented me with a picture of Princess Di shortly after she'd given birth to Harry: 'I wan' rook rike that,' she said. The beloved Royal's hair was slightly below shoulder-length at the time, and the picture my client gave me with such hope and trust showed it swept up at the back, with plenty of bouncy body in the front, and topped by a tiara.

Well, I like a challenge, and two hours and two full cans of hairspray later, I can honestly say that my client's hair bore a reasonable resemblance to Di's. I didn't have a tiara to complete the look, but I've seldom been prouder of a 'do.

I'm afraid we did take the piss a bit out of the Japanese obsession with politeness. Once a client was done, she would bow prettily and murmur, 'Doumo arigatou.' We would bow back and say, 'Doumo arigatou.' She would immediately bow back, with thanks. And we would do the same. And so would she. And so would we.

By this time our client would be backing out of the salon, still bowing and thanking us. And we would – sometimes all twelve of us – be bowing back, with many heartfelt thanks. Sometimes we managed to bow-and-thank clients all the way down the corridor.

The Jean Ann Ryan singers and dancers, who were required to perform a dinner cabaret twice a night in the Queen's Room – an early and a late sitting – for an exhausting run of six weeks during this mooring, also got pretty damned fed up and decided to have a bit of fun. The words of their first act, 'Masquerade', from the Andrew Lloyd Webber musical *Phantom of the Opera*, with people dancing and swirling about in costumes, were, 'Masquerade! Paper faces on parade…' The singers changed these opening lines to, 'Masquerade! Getting pissed and getting laid…' We knew it was childish, but we'd all fall about laughing, holding our stomachs and clutching each other, when the Japanese audience applauded enthusiastically at the end of the number.

Back in port, we were once again on 'bar cashier' duty, and one of the perks of the job was that the hours weren't too long or onerous – which gave us plenty of time to explore the area surrounding the port. We quickly became regulars at a hole in the wall called the Oozo Bar, presided over by Mama-san and her large, mannish offspring, Daughter-san (whom we suspected may have begun life as Son-san). Here, we downed peach-schnapps shooters and ordered meals of varying quality (delicious when drunk; dubious when sober).

Once, when Mama-san ran out of peach schnapps, some bright spark decided the time had come to sample a bottle of alcohol that always stood in pride of place behind the bar: it was clear spirit, and in it was suspended a dead reptile of some kind.

'What's that?' we asked Mama-san.

'That Gecko,' she replied. 'It velly, velly old. It velly, velly good.'

It was all the encouragement we needed. Over the course of the next hour, we ordered four Geckoes each. My memory is admittedly not all it should be concerning that evening, but I remember it indeed being 'velly, velly good' – so good, in fact, that some time later, tripping out of our skulls on whatever was in that bottle (rocket fuel, perhaps; or maybe formaldehyde), we helped ourselves to a couple of bicycles that were parked outside the bar and cycled insanely up and down the harbour.

The next night we were back for more – in spite of black-dog babbelas all round, we were keen for another Gecko-fuelled experience and returned to have another go at the special bottle. So we were a little disappointed to find it in its usual place – but with its level up, once again, to the very top. Whatever we'd been drinking hadn't, apparently, been magically infused over many years by essence-of-gecko.

(I told one of my favourite clients this story shortly after the incident. In the next port of call, she came back on board with a cloth gecko she'd bought at a market. 'Here, lizard-breath,' she said, presenting it to me. I *loved* passengers whose sense of humour was as warped as mine.)

On one of these forays to the Oozo Bar we took with us a young public-room steward. Brian was about to turn 19 and had foolishly let slip that he was still a virgin, and obviously this was not a state of affairs that any of us were prepared to allow to continue. After some discussion with Mama-san and Daughter-san, it was agreed that Daughter-san be given the honour of deflowering the young man (for a fee, of course).

Daughter-san seemed delighted at the prospect, and willingly hid behind a curtain while we brought Brian in to the bar to present him with his birthday surprise. At the appointed time, Daughter-san emerged, looking even more like a Samurai warrior than usual, her arms outstretched in welcome towards Brian.

Brian's reaction was immediate and, at first, amusing: he began hyperventilating and shot into the men's room. We all fell about laughing, then I went to coax him out. The door was locked. I knocked. I could hear Brian in there, wheezing like a bellows. 'Hey, buddy, you okay?' I asked.

He wasn't. We didn't know that Brian was asthmatic and the shock of the prospect of having his cherry popped by

Daughter-san had triggered an attack. By the time we broke open the door, Brian was prostrate and turning purple.

We got Brian back to the ship in time for treatment and he recovered fully. But he never came out with us again.

§

Barmen in the hospitality industry are notorious swordsmen – women find them, like drummers, irresistible – and it was no different on the *QE2*. One of these was an Irishman called Gerald who, in spite of not being notably attractive, somehow contrived always to have at least two girlfriends on the boil.

Two in particular, both regulars on the liner, were a 30something called Sue-Anne and a 60something called Maxine. What Maxine lacked in youth she more than made up for in glamour: she was always dressed to the nines and immaculately groomed, and her crowning glories were a range of stunning wigs.

Gerald had been bonking both of these women for several years – often when they were simultaneously on board. But in a floating village like the *QE2*, it was inevitable that secrets will out, and this particular one exploded into a vicious catfight. Maxine was sitting in the Lido one night, making eyes at her lover across the bar and sipping on a cocktail, when Sue-Anne burst in, eyes blazing and fingernails extended. The battle that ensued was both a bit frightening and rather funny, but poor Maxine took the brunt of it: Sue-Anne's coup de grace was snatching the wig from her rival's head and hurling it across the room.

Maxine slunk away, humiliated, and I never saw her on board again. Sue-Anne wasted no time in sealing her victory by marrying Gerald and whisking him away to the safety of her stately pile in Bloomfield Hills, Michigan – one of the top five wealthiest cities in the USA and home to personages the likes of Lee Iacocca, actress Selma Blair and billionaire William Arnoldson. There, she put him in charge of her estate and her two delinquent children before resuming her globetrotting lifestyle.

Perhaps not surprisingly, it wasn't long before Sue-Anne was once again on the *QE2* – and once again in the Lido, making eyes at Gerald's replacement, a Mexican called Cesar. This was where I came into the picture: because Gerald knew me and, probably because I was gay and therefore not sexual competition for him, he trusted me, he put me 'in charge' of Sue-Anne while she was on board. Big mistake: Sue-Anne was a wild child and even if I'd wanted to (which I most certainly didn't), I wouldn't have been able to babysit her.

This was a woman who would sashay into the Lido, look around for a likely candidate and, without batting an eyelid (other than in a provocative way, of course), walk over to him and say, 'Fancy a fuck?'

Sue-Anne was a very attractive woman and it was rare she was turned down. But things became a little more complicated when she began adding, 'Okay if my friend joins us?' and inviting me to the party.

Gerald, stashed on the estate in Michigan, knew something was going on. He would phone the ship at all hours of the day and night, furious and desperate, threatening Sue-Anne, Cesar and me with dismemberment and/or death. Inevitably, Sue-Anne finally had enough of Gerald and cut him free with a hefty divorce settlement.

As for me, I eventually spent over a year in Bloomfield Hills, Michigan, myself – as Sue-Anne's personal hairdresser. When word went out that I'd accepted her offer to go and live with her, I received postcards and telexes from friends all over the world to enquire whether I'd gone straight. The fact was, I hadn't, but my penis had: as much as I liked to think I wasn't available for purchase, my member decided of its own accord that it wanted to live like the rich and famous. It took me sixteen months to persuade it that there was more to life than Lear jets and limousines.

The scale of the wealth of some of the *QE2*'s passengers was difficult for 'ordinary' folk like us to appreciate, but Sue-Anne's mission to find a lavender jade Buddha goes some way to illustrating this. Jade in its classic green is particularly valuable in the east – roughly comparable to gold and diamonds in the west. Sue-Anne's wish, however, was for a 'lavender' jade statuette – she liked the delicate violet shade of that form of the gemstone.

After a long night of peach schnapps and champagne, I accompanied Sue-Anne to a jade house in Singapore to find her Buddha. We were both somewhat dishevelled and, I daresay, reeked of old alcohol, so the delightfully named Miss Fun, the clerk who helped us, was less than keen to take out her top-of-the-range 'laughing Buddha' statues. After much persuasion and assurance, however, she finally did, and showed Sue-Anne a piece priced at $50 000.

'No, no, Miss Fun, you can't be serious!' Sue-Anne said, a touch hysterically, and Miss Fun's face dropped – clearly, we were just tourists wasting her time. But she cheered up again when Sue-Anne said, 'I won't pay a cent more than $25 000 for that one.'

Sue-Anne walked out the jade house that day with four lavender Jade Buddha statuettes which together cost her about $50 000. Not bad for a half-hour's shopping spree.

(Many years later, when I was back in South Africa and Sue-Anne in the US, she phoned me and told me about an evening she'd had at a strip club in New Orleans, where she'd unwittingly racked up a hefty bill, paying, for herself and two male guests, for a practically endless stream of Cristal champagne, a series of high-charging lap dancers and a private room that was – unknown to her, she said – hired out at a staggering per-hour basis. When she told me what her bill had come to, I almost got sick: here in South Africa, I could have used the money she'd paid to buy a house and a car for cash, and still have change left over. By then I'd left the excesses of the *QE2* far behind me, and all I could ask her was, 'Are you bragging or are you complaining?')

Another of Sue-Anne's hairbrained schemes while on the ship was her 'massages around the world' mission: she was intent on having a massage in every port of call. I accompanied her on many of these excursions. In Japan we couldn't find a masseur and opted instead to go to a local, highly recommended physiotherapist, who worked us over so thoroughly that both of us had trouble walking for days afterwards. Our Hong Kong experience stands out for the simple reason that we were continually offered 'extras'.

But the best massage Sue-Anne got was in Manila, where we were directed to a very down-at-heel-looking hairdressing salon. There, a masseur called Raoul invited Sue-Anne to step into 'the back' – literally, simply a corner at the back of the salon screened off from view by a tatty curtain. I sat in the reception area, listening to Sue-Anne's screams of pleasure. 'Oooh, Raoul! Oooh, Raoul!' she kept moaning.

When at last she emerged, pink-faced and loose-limbed, from behind the curtain, it was to a salon full of saucer-eyed Filipino women. We didn't hang around to see what happened subsequently, but I wouldn't be surprised if Raoul experienced a sudden rush of willing customers.

Sue-Anne's brother, Harold, was another frequent cruiser and became a friend of the crew. Harold was autistic and had some 'savant' skills; because this was around the time of the release of the movie *Rain Man*, starring Dustin Hoffman as autistic savant Raymond Babbitt and Tom Cruise as his selfish, yuppie brother Charlie, Harold inevitably became known as 'Rain Man'.

The first we knew of Harold's unusual facility with numbers was when he, I and two other crew members went ashore in the Seychelles. We decided to hire a car for the day. Because none of us was earning fabulous salaries, the usual practice was to split the cost of the car hire and the fuel between whoever was using it.

We pulled into a gas station to refuel the car. I was driving and I asked the petrol jockey to put in 10 gallons of petrol. The exchange rate at the time was around 5,5 Seychelles rupees was to the American dollar; fuel cost about $1 per gallon. We had rupees but, new to the place, we weren't at all au fait with conversions.

'That's 13,75 rupees each,' said Harold immediately, apparently without having calculated a thing.

We ignored him and continued to bicker and squabble over the calculator – we were hairstylists, not mathematicians, and our combined maths skills probably wouldn't have impressed a junior-school learner. But ten difficult minutes later, we arrived at the answer: 13,75 rupees each.

We all turned to Harold in amazement. 'How did you do that?' I asked.

He, in his turn, ignored me. Rocking excitedly, he asked, 'Where are the birdies?' 'Birdies' was Harold's name for prostitutes – he'd been introduced to some friendly whores and their tricks of the trade at an earlier stopover, and his only goal became to find 'birdies' in every subsequent port of call.

Harold's other 'savant' skill was in music – his father was a bigwig in the music business and he'd been exposed to all kinds of music from early in his life. His encyclopaedic knowledge never failed to amaze and impress us. '"Proud Mary",' someone would prompt him, and Harold, rocking away with his eyes closed, would recite, 'Written by John Fogerty, recorded by Creedence Clearwater Revival, released 15 January 1969, 3.07 minutes long, covered by Status Quo, Ike and Tina Turner, Della Reese.'

'"We built this city",' someone else would say, challengingly, and Harold would recite, 'Written by Bernie Taupin, recorded by Starship, Mickey Thomas and Grace Slick on lead vocals, released 10 November 1985, 4.56 minutes long, got to number one in the US and number 12 in the UK.'

Harold called me 'The Marlboro Man' because I smoked Marlboro cigarettes, and he displayed another uncanny ability: If I even *thought* I wanted a cigarette, Harold would suddenly appear at my shoulder, packet extended in one hand, with a cigarette poking out and ready for plucking, and lighter in the other. I must say, it sometimes creeped me out.

§

One barman who never charged me for a drink was Pedro – for the simple reason that I saved his life. This happened in Rio de Janeiro in Brazil, when we were on shore leave taking in the sights. We'd been atop the Corcovado (named one of the New Seven Wonders of the World in 2007), admired the gigantic statue of Christ the Redeemer at its summit, and had then gone up the Sugarloaf by cable car. We had, as was usual when we went ashore, been drinking fairly steadily all day and by this time neither of us was anywhere near sober.

'Snap me, snap me!' Pedro shouted, clowning around. He struck a pose, leaning back against a railing – which made an ominous creaking sound and suddenly gave way.

I don't know what instinct was at work in me that day, but I lunged forward, shot out a hand and grabbed his shirt. Pedro hung teetering over the 500-metre sheer drop into the ravine below for several seconds before I managed to haul him back to safety.

Another reason Rio sticks in my mind was for the madness around its carnival, which has been a yearly highlight on the city's calendar since the 1930s. But Rio – where many of the infamous slums are located right next to the wealthier areas – is also known as one of the most violent cities in the world, and the cruise director made no bones about this on our first stop there, when he told us to not only carry our money in our shoes, but also to remove every single bit of visible jewellery. 'Yes, stud earrings too,' he said, when someone asked – 'unless you want your earlobes pulled off.'

He wasn't wrong. As I joined the throngs of celebrants on the world-famous Copacabana, I was at first alarmed and then simply disbelieving at the number of strange hands that delved into my pockets, shot down my trousers and groped around inside my shirt.

8. Below Decks

Keeping the *QE2*'s passengers fed, watered and otherwise nurtured and cared for during the 109-day world cruise was a feat of astonishing logistical organisation. This floating village became famous for going through, for instance, 2 500 tea bags and 3 000 eggs *per day*. In a week, the ship's inhabitants would consume over 1 000 kg each of bacon and chicken, about 7 000 kg of fresh vegetables and 3 000 kg of fruit, around 1 000 kg of sugar and over 2 000 bottles of wine. The annual list of luxury consumables included about 20 000 kg of lobster, 1 000 kg of caviar (the *QE2* was the largest consumer of caviar on earth) and 73 000 bottles of champagne.

Although when the ship left Southampton, its stocks were fully replenished, New York City was one of the stopovers where top-ups were necessary, to restock the ship for either its return voyage across the Atlantic or its onward journey on the world cruise. There, the grocery list included 250 kg of coffee, 43 000 eggs, 220 kg of mayonnaise, over 1 000 kg of butter, 2 500 metres of aluminium foil and 15 000 cocktail stirrers. The telex requisitioning food supplies that was forwarded to Cunard's headquarters in New York ahead of the ship's landing there was sometimes over four metres long.

Not only this, but 2 000 tons of fresh water and 3 000 tons of fuel were taken on – the water supplies were supplemented by the *QE2*'s evaporators, which produced about 900 additional tons of fresh water daily; and the ship's fuel oil tank capacity of just over 4 000 tons was sufficient for ten days' sailing, about 7 800 miles.

The Coast Guard also had to complete a full inspection of the ship's safety equipment, including lowering the lifeboats. And, on the trans-Atlantic runs, some 1 800 passengers might have to be checked out and another 1 800 checked in, necessitating a turnaround of upwards of 5 000 pieces of luggage.

The ship seldom overnighted in New York, apparently because of the gigantic docking fees, which ran to about $100 000 per day in the early 1980s. Turnaround time in New York was usually around nine hours, but this was determined by the efficiency (or otherwise) of the longshoremen there, whose job it was to offload and onload baggage and take on board all provisions. It was, notably, during a longshoremen's strike in 1986 that the *QE2* made it into the *Guinness Book of Records* – for quickest turnaround time, breaking the existing record by nine minutes. The ship arrived in New York at 5pm and, fully restocked and with a full passenger complement, sailed again just five hours and 38 minutes later. 'This was only achieved by a combined effort of the *QE2*'s officers and crew, together with the entire New York office staff,' general manager TJ Conroy said at the time. He wasn't exaggerating – hairdressers, waiters, shop assistants, chefs and cabin stewards became temporary longshoremen, hustling across the picket line.

It was also in New York, some years later – in 2007, after my time – that the nasty norovirus stomach bug was said to have come on board. This virus, which causes vomiting and diarrhoea, had infected more than 270 passengers and about thirty crew members by the time the ship arrived in Mexico (the norovirus loves cruise ships – all those people in a confined space is exactly what it needs to spread). In an effort to control the outbreak, the captain confined all victims to their cabins, cancelled all cocktail parties and banned self-service items from the buffet; he also supervised a total sanitation programme of the ship after disembarking all the passengers.

Leaving New York was always very emotional: the ship would sail down the Hudson River, passing the World Trade Centre, and, about fifteen minutes later, the Statue of Liberty; passengers would throng the decks, taking pictures, cheering and sometimes quite literally in tears of rapture. It was one of the times the *QE2* felt, perhaps, most regal: this ambulatory world icon, paying its respects to some of the most recognised landmarks on the planet.

But one of the characteristics of much of the *QE2* staff was how much they liked taking the piss, and the tone of one of these poignant leave-takings was considerably lowered by a group of on-board photographers, who'd nipped onshore beforehand and bought themselves a blow-up doll that they called Miranda. They inflated the hapless Miranda with helium gas from a handy bottle kept in the photography studio, and tied her to one of the ship's aft flagpoles before our departure. So, while we sailed in a stately manner away from one of the most famous cities in all the world, and into the mighty Atlantic, Miranda, her bright red lips pouting and her pink plastic legs splayed, bobbed along behind us.

§

In 1994 the *QE2* had a large-scale refit – one of many during its lifetime, but this one stood out because it was, not to put too fine a point on it, an utter disaster. Aimed at revitalising the 'hotel' part of the ship, it cost Cunard $45 million (£30 million) and was every bit as ambitious as the 1986 technical overhaul that changed the ship's propulsion system from steam to diesel-electric.

Included on the long list of changes were the conversion of the Quarter Deck pool area into a permanent dining venue, the Lido buffet; the creation of the Crystal Bar; and the transformation of the Midships Bar into the Chart Room. Some of the more expensive cabins were also to be upgraded, and the bathrooms in all the passenger cabins were to be given a full refurbishment.

Trouble began almost immediately when some workmen came on board in Fort Lauderdale, when the ship was still completing its last world cruise before the refit, and there were several passenger complaints about wolf-whistles and demeaning comments made as they passed these rough-and-readies hanging out at various spots on the deck. The ship offloaded the last of its paying passengers in New York, then sailed sans passengers to Hamburg in Germany, where most of the work was to be done.

During refits there was always a Steiner representative on board, and it was usually the company's maritime manager, Mr Beckwith, a hideous little person who favoured grey suits and pink ties and had what he probably thought was 'an eye for the ladies' but was in fact a sickeningly sleazy attitude to women, and bimbos in particular. He would use these bits of fluff to get work done in the salon, sending a pretty little someone, for instance, to negotiate with a recalcitrant but horny plumber.

For this refit, however, Mr Beckwith topped himself, deputising in his place a Steiner representative who appeared to be in training for princessdom. Cecelia came up to Mr James's usual standards of prettiness but had in addition an attitude that wouldn't have gone amiss at Buck House. This was a package that, unfortunately, proved irresistible to the overall project manager of the refit, one Mr Nowicki, who wasted no time abandoning his new wife of only three months (she had stayed behind in New York) and beginning a hot and heavy affair with Princess Cecelia, with disastrous consequences for the work. The pussy-struck Mr Nowicki spent so much time romancing his new girlfriend that he left precious few minutes over for managing the project for which he had been employed.

By the time the *QE2* sailed out of Hamburg in preparation for picking up passengers for the next world cruise, the work was far from finished – and that which had been done, had been done badly. For the first few weeks of the cruise, passengers rubbed shoulders with over 2 000 orange-overalled workmen of every conceivable nationality as they battled to finish the refit. (I heard at least one story of a knifing in one of the public rooms; we suspected at the time that many of the 'artisans' on board had been recruited from German prisoner-release programmes!)

One of the swimming pools was fenced off and unusable, and the big-screen cinema showings had to be cancelled after it was discovered that the projector had been hit with a hammer. For the first few days, there was no laundry or valet service. Burst pipes flooded cabins, and some passengers had to be supplied with blankets so they could sleep in the corridors. Escape routes were blocked and safety doors missing or not working, and building materials littered the decks and corridors.

As if that weren't bad enough, the bathrooms had been left until last, and the work on the plumbing that was most shoddily done. Passengers complained of pools of dirty water in the bathrooms, and one lady passenger whose flush button, rather than safely whirling away her leavings, instead spat them straight back into her face, made it her business to find out exactly who was responsible for this monumental fuckup. By the time she discovered that it was Mr Nowicki, we were in Aruba in the southern Caribbean, and that hapless man was sitting in a restaurant with Princess Cecelia, cooing sweet nothings in her ear.

The lady passenger, the memory of having to wipe shit out of her eyes still clearly fresh in her mind, marched over to the happy couple. 'Are you Mr Nowicki?' she demanded.

He tore his attention away from his lady-love long enough to look up and murmur, 'Yes. Can I help you?'

The lady passenger didn't bother to answer. Instead, she snotklapped him so hard she knocked him right out of his chair.

Even Prince Andrew, who served in the Royal Navy and probably knew a bit about ships, remarked on the premature return to business-as-usual of the *QE2* after this refit. On board for a celebratory lunch in Southampton at which he was a guest of honour, he learnt that the ship hadn't gone through sea trials before sailing back from Hamburg to Southampton. 'Sea trials' are the testing phase of any watercraft and take place on open water. They're conducted to measure a vessel's performance and general seaworthiness and test things like speed, manoeuvrability, equipment and safety features. This royal personage actually commented to me, 'You're a braver man than I – I certainly wouldn't have gone in an unproven vessel across the North Sea.' (The sea trials ultimately took place in Southampton before the ship departed on its disastrous journey to New York.)

Proving that no publicity is bad publicity, however, that tour – dubbed by some 'Fawlty Towers Afloat' – attracted a gigantic popular following, as people flocked to ports in various countries to have a look at 'the cruise ship from hell'. That Christmas cruise ultimately cost Cunard about £7.5 million in compensation payouts – and its chief executive, John Olsen, who resigned in the wake of the scandal.

§

From a practical point of view, the ship was broken down into three divisions: the 'engineering' department, which made sure the ship worked properly as an oceangoing vessel; the 'hotel' side of things, which catered for the hospitality requirements of the passengers; and the concessionaires – photographers, hairstylists, boutique staff, etc – who were employed by companies separate from the shipping line.

At sea, maritime law came first and foremost, and the captain was in ultimate control of everyone on board, regardless of where in this 'ranking' they fell (passengers included). So, for instance, while Steiner staff fell under the auspices of Steiner while on land, the ship's captain was our 'boss' when we were at sea – although we were directly answerable to the hotel manager, who in turn was answerable to the staff captain, who reported to the captain.

All staff and crew were required to undertake training to ensure that we knew exactly how to conduct ourselves on board ship: we had regular emergency drills, for instance, and were taught how to help passengers into life jackets and direct them to the lifeboats. Then, in order to do our jobs up to the standard required, we had to learn the rules of five-star hotel service – not only how to conduct ourselves around passengers, but also personal presentation including neat haircuts, clean nails and immaculate uniforms. And, finally, every port of call had different rules and regulations (mainly concerning hygiene) that had to be adhered to. So the glamour of working on the *QE2* was offset by the fact that our jobs weren't restricted to just what we'd nominally been employed to do: there was much nitty-gritty besides.

The emergency drills were part and parcel of every embarkation, and over the twelve years I worked on the *QE2*, I did hundreds of them. When we knew it was just a drill, things went smoothly. The one time when it wasn't, however, I realised how genuine danger can sow panic and disorder, and how necessary these drills really were.

Fortunately, this near-disaster happened when the ship was in dry dock in Hamburg for its refit, and no passengers were aboard. A dry dock is a narrow basin that can be flooded to allow a vessel in, then drained so that the ship comes to rest on blocks. This is done for both routine cleaning (such as the removal of barnacles and rust) and for repairs and maintenance. Once the work is finished, the dock is re-flooded and the ship carefully refloated.

The port of Hamburg is situated about 100 kilometres upriver from the mouth of the Elbe, and that's where the *QE2* was docked, in Elbe 17, also known as Blohm & Voss, one of the biggest floating (or movable) dry docks in Europe. Downriver, at the mouth, there was a berth where container ships were moored – this very busy port handled up to ten million containers a year.

It was the small hours of the morning and I was fast asleep in my cabin down on 5 Deck. We'd been in dry dock for a couple of days and, with no passengers on board, there had been plenty of time to party.

When the tannoy crackled to life, it took me a few panicky moments to work out where I was: there were little men pounding drums in my head and my mouth felt like a camel had died in it.

'Abandon ship! Abandon ship! Abandon ship! This is not a drill! Repeat, this is not a drill!'

The captain's voice rang urgently in my ears as I scrabbled around my cabin, trying to find the door. The power was off. It was December, the very middle of the European winter, and the dark was dense and all-encompassing.

Finally, I located the door and flung it open. I looked up and down the corridor but there wasn't so much as a glimmer of light; I heard and felt, rather than saw, people running and shouting. The 'remain calm' invocation had been completely forgotten.

I stumbled out, dressed only in trackpants and a vest. The cold was biting but adrenaline had started to push through my body and I didn't register it – yet. I lurched up the corridor, banging into walls and people, all of us trying to find a way out.

By feel, I found a staircase and struggled up it. I followed a throng of people as we made our way up through the decks of the ship. We were all trying to find a gangway off, but the location of these was different now that we were in dry dock, and the panic deepened as we shouted to each other – 'Here! This way!' 'No, this way!'

Finally, more by luck than anything else, a mob of us burst out into the open air. The lights of the dry dock outside were blinding, and the sight that greeted us was brightly lit, like a bad dream. Close by – not more than fifty metres away – was the looming bulk of a container ship... and it was drifting closer. The gigantically heavy *QE2*, weighing over 70 000 tons, was balanced on blocks, and if the container ship made contact with it, it was sure to go over.

Despite our training in emergency drills and the oft-repeated order to 'walk, not run', we dashed frenziedly down the gangway onto the dry dock, and from there made our way to dry land. We huddled in the freezing night air, asking each other what had happened. Slowly the story emerged: a freak wind down at the river mouth had caused some of the container ships to break their moorings, and they had drifted upriver towards the main port.

We were herded into a nearby warehouse, where the purser started taking roll call. By 8am everyone was accounted for and the rogue container ship had been secured and towed to safety.

By now the shock was wearing off. We were laughing about our brush with disaster – but we were also freezing our arses off. It was below zero outside and most of us had fled our cabins wearing only what we'd pulled on to sleep in. It had been drummed into us that 'warm clothes, life jackets and medications are important in an "abandon ship" situation', but there wasn't one among us who had heeded this. It was obvious to all what we needed: alcohol, and lots of it.

We summoned taxis and soon a gaggle of inappropriately dressed *QE2* crew was heading for the Reeperbahn, Hamburg's red-light district, located conveniently near the harbour. ('Reeper' comes, in fact, from the old Low German word for 'ship's rope' – the red-light district started life as a 'ropewalk' where heavy ropes were produced.) Here, in 'die sündige Meile' (the sinful mile), we followed that old seaman's tradition of celebrating our survival and drowning our fears.

§

The *QE2*, like any ship at sea, is obliged to respond to mayday messages sent out by other vessels, and in August 1990, with a full payload of passengers en route to Bergen in Norway, we responded to one. In a Force 9 northwest wind in the notoriously temperamental North Sea, the Norwegian oil-drilling platform West Gamma send out an SOS: the rig's accommodation platform was adrift with 49 people on board;

its helicopter landing platform had been destroyed, along with some of its lifesaving appliances.

Because of the rig's pitching and rolling, lifeboats couldn't be launched, and with the helipad out of action, evacuation by air was also impossible. The *QE2* was requested to proceed to the area, 47 miles away, and act as an on-scene rescue commander. Although it was by this time 2 in the morning, the captain, Ronald Warwick – the same master who'd seen us safely through Hurricane Luis some years before – made frequent tannoy broadcasts to tell the passengers what was happening.

By 4am the *QE2* was near the rig. Those passengers who weren't in their bunks were instructed by Warwick to sit down and hold tight, so that he could turn the huge vessel into the wind, to position it so it could launch its lifeboats – but then Warwick was told, inexplicably, that the crew of the rig didn't wish to be evacuated. With the *QE2* summarily and without explanation released from its duties as rescue commander, Warwick had no choice but to continue to Bergen.

The next morning we learnt that the rig had capsized and sunk, and that the crew had had to tie themselves together in groups and jump into the sea. Four rescue craft despatched by the Danes had picked them up, although one of these vessels itself had capsized.

Although no lives were lost, an on-site seaman said after the event that the risk to the crew would have been lessened had 'the UK practice of using two tugs and an auxiliary vessel been used'. We never learnt why the services of the *QE2* – an 'auxiliary vessel' if ever there were one, right there, and with all hands on deck and ready to help – weren't gratefully received.

(Interestingly, while researching this event for this book, using an extract of the *QE2* logbook – which minutely details the ship's movements from 12h00 on 20 August until 20h00 the following day – we could find no other record of the *QE2*'s putative involvement in this rescue. One of the Danish sea-rescue service vessels that picked up the crewmen who finally jumped off the rig did, however, win an international safety award for the rescue!)

§

'Rapid searches' following bomb threats were another regular feature for crew, taking place about once a month. For these exercises, a 'suspicious package' would be concealed somewhere on the ship and the staff would then be informed of the 'bomb threat' and tasked with finding the object. We were under the strictest of instructions never to touch the package; we were simply to quickly report its whereabouts to the nearest officer.

Although no real incendiary device was ever found on board, the ship did experience a real bomb scare in 1972. Although it turned out to be a hoax, the crew did a rapid search, then a bomb-disposal team was quickly summoned and parachuted into the sea nearby. This incident was said to have inspired the 1974 movie *Juggernaut*.

And one crew member was declared a 'fatality' after one of our rapid-search drills. The fittingly named Lionel Mort ('mort' is French for 'death'), a hapless hairdresser, once found a package he thought was suspicious. Or was it? Despite the strict instructions to the contrary, he figured there was only one way to find out, and he picked it up. It 'exploded' in his face, covering him with tell-tale white powder.

There was, however, a real threat of terrorist action against the ship, during a 1987 charter in Boston – a city with a substantial population of Irish descent during the height of the civil war in Ireland.

A few years earlier, three Massachusetts men had been convicted of smuggling weapons and ammunition for the Irish Republican Army and sentenced to up to ten years in prison. Two Boston citizens, Joseph Paul Murray Junior and Patrick Nee, had bought the cache – 163 firearms, 11 bulletproof vests, 71 000 rounds of ammunition, rockets and hand grenades – and Robert Anderson of Gloucester had used his trawler to transport them. The haul, the largest IRA-bound arms in more than a decade, was seized off Ireland.

Not that this was in the minds of the 25 000 people who attended Digital Equipment Corporation's ten-day DECWorld '87 exhibition, one of the drawcards of which was the docking of the *QE2* – a quintessentially British icon – next to Boston's World Trade Centre, to act as a floating hotel. A cost of a cabin was comparable to a room in one of Boston's first-class hotels – from $185 to $335 per night – and the *QE2* also served lunches, held cocktail parties and ran its regular programme of entertainment. The organisers turned handsprings over the success of the exhibition, saying that the *QE2* had 'added pizzazz' to the occasion.

Behind the scenes, of course, we were all working our butts off as usual – but there were extra personnel brought in, people who worked every bit as hard and whom none of the exhibition attendees knew about: teams of divers who went down in twenty-minute intervals to sweep around the bottom of the ship for explosive devices.

A memory of Boston – a centre of learning, with several universities and colleges within the city and surrounds – is how strict the nightclubs and pubs were about not allowing underage people in, and how overtly homophobic the student population seemed to be. I was often asked to produce proof of my age – 27 at the time – before being admitted to a club, which I thought vaguely entertaining (and sometimes, when I'd forgotten to take along my ID, enormously irritating). Not so amusing, however, was when a group of men from the ship got on the dance floor together. English blokes loved to dance, and so did I – something our American brothers thought terrifically namby-pamby, and particularly so when we danced *with each other*. More than once we had to scarper for our lives when we were threatened with grievous bodily harm for being moffies.

§

The *QE2* had four galleys, one for each restaurant; two of these were open round the clock for room service. To give you some idea of the scale of the fit-out of the kitchens and dining rooms, this is what was to be found in their stock rooms: 51 000 items of glassware, 64 000 items of crockery,

36 000 items of cutlery, 8 000 items of kitchenware and 64 000 items of tableware.

The crew weren't strictly allowed in any of the galleys but when coming off duty or leaving a party in the early hours of the morning with a bit of a hunger going, they were the obvious place to go. They became an informal dark-hours meeting point, and more than once I got two late-night takeaways there: a club sandwich and a willing crew member.

A galley chef who stands out in my memory was a man whose name was Larry but who went by the more descriptive moniker 'Dizzie'. This flamboyant homosexual would, from time to time, get a team together to play darts against the engineers. The two teams couldn't have been more different: Dizzie's team – 'Dizzie's Diamantés' – dressed in drag from the shoulders up; and the engineers, who certainly didn't bother with a team costume, and came with the sole intention of winning the darts championship.

Ultimately, the engineers didn't have a prayer. The mood was always slightly hysterical and often hysterically over-the-top. Dizzie's team was made up of mad gay men, all of whom went by showgirl names (Shanella, Doris, Dolores, etc) and who spoke a complicated and exclusively gay lingo – for instance, the apparently nonsensical 'Vada the slap on that cod eek' meant 'Look at the makeup on that ugly face'. Not only that, but the women who came to cheer on the teams made no secret of their bias towards Dizzie's Diamantés and weren't above doing some covert cheating for 'their girls'. No matter how carefully the engineers chose their team or how cleverly they played, they always lost.

The laundry – run and managed by eighteen Chinese nationals – never slept. Not only did it deal with the uncountable loads of linen coming in from the cabins and restaurants every day, it also took care, on a same-day basis, of passengers' clothes (including dry-cleaning and specialist cleaning of designer gowns) and, of course, the crew's uniforms. On a normal trans-Atlantic voyage, this laundry would process 3 000 table cloths, 1 000 oven cloths, 3 000 pillow cases, thousands of sheets and blankets, over 20 000 towels, and around 3 000 bags of general laundry. (A massive compliment to the laundry came via my mother, the world's most exacting laundress: 'Who does your laundry?' she asked, in frank admiration, the first time she saw me in my uniform.)

This vast quantity of washing required an enormous amount of organisation, and it was the job of Mr Chu, who headed up the laundry, to correctly tag every dirty load that came in. That was always where I found him when I took down my bag of laundry: sitting at the front counter, tagging.

I'd say to him, 'Hi, Mr Chu, how are you?'

And he always had the same answer: 'I'm fine. It's those *other* fuckers…'

The real hats-off to the laundry was the fact that, cleaning identical uniforms for over a thousand crew members, it very seldom happened that someone ended up wearing a jacket, for instance, that was clearly way too big or too small for them.

§

The *QE2* had a five-slot morgue on board and, due to the age and occasional infirmity of some of its passengers, it wasn't unusual for at least some of these slots to be filled from time to time. On one world cruise they were *all* filled – with crew members, one of whom had died of a sudden heart attack and two of drug overdoses.

Although I don't remember any burials at sea from my time on the ship, I do recall a story told by Captain Alan Bennell, a much-loved master whose tenure was cut short when he died of stomach cancer. Captain Bennell told of officiating, as the first mate on the *QE2*, the scattering at sea of the ashes of a merchant marine. Inexperienced at the time, he didn't allow for the wind direction when he was instructed by the captain, with a discreet nod of his head, to toss the ashes. He threw them forwards, then turned to face to the captain – who was lightly coated in grey from crown to shoulders.

Quietly, Bennell said to the captain, 'Whatever you do, sir, don't lick your lips.'

It was just after my time that Bob Muller, then aged 85, died on the ship. He'd contracted a virus that was difficult to treat because he had emphysema; he could have been disembarked and signed into a hospital but Mr Muller, then on his fifth world cruise on the *QE2* with his wife Beatrice, elected to die on board. Mr Muller's body was kept in the morgue until the ship docked in Southampton, where one of his sons collected it and accompanied it home to the USA for cremation.

This story is particularly interesting because of Beatrice – who elected after her husband's death to stay on the ship until it completed its world cruise, and then went one step further: she sold all she owned and moved permanently onto the *QE2*.

Bob's ashes were consigned to the sea as the ship left Los Angeles some months later. As for Bea: by the time the *QE2* was decommissioned in 2008, she was aged 89 and had lived on board in retirement for fourteen years, at a cost of some £3 500 per month. Asked what her plans were, she said, 'I just want to find another place that has ballroom dancing, duplicate bridge and some lovely ports — and a lot of nice people and good food.'

9. The Bridge

There's no quite so fine a sight as a ship's officer all tricked out in his whites. From his jaunty cap and shoulder epaulettes down to his mirror-shiny shoes, he represents all that women (and many men) find so alluring about a man in uniform.

This sexual trump card wasn't lost on the officers, many of whom were married but who took advantage nonetheless – as did so many of our passengers – of being afloat in a self-contained little world, far from the probing eyes and suspicious questions of wives and girlfriends.

Which made for interesting times when, a couple of months a year, the wives of the married officers came on board to join their husbands. There was a pecking order among the wives, of course – the higher the rank of the husband, the higher the wife ranked among the women; and some of these women were so enamoured of their own status that they thought their shit didn't stink.

It was these I listened to with special attention when, while I was blowdrying or colouring or cutting their hair, they told me about their perfect husbands. One wife in particular made heavy work of her flawless relationship with her spouse – blissfully unaware that it was common knowledge among the crew that his preference was for male waiters and, more specifically, sex with them in front of a full-length mirror.

Another married officer – a little troll of a man – pursued me relentlessly for the ten years we both worked on board. At crew parties I would be aware of him watching me and keeping track of how much I was drinking; then, when he judged I was pissed enough, he'd sidle over and proposition me.

Once, in a moment of regrettable weakness, I acquiesced. He gave me an oily grin. 'Meet me in my cabin in fifteen minutes,' he said, sliding away.

Too blind-drunk to care about the consequences, I followed a few moments later. When he opened the door, I was treated to the sight of not only the troll in the altogether, but four waiters too – all butt-naked. I beat a hasty retreat. (They weren't very nice waiters.)

While we cruise staff didn't have much time for the merchant officers – despite their fancy uniforms, we'd remind ourselves, most of them would be nothing more than vacuum-cleaner salesmen on land – they were much loved by the women passengers. One such was the somewhat pathetic estranged wife of a retail magnate whom I shall call Mrs Q. Mrs Q, whose husband had discovered that he would lose a great deal of his amassed fortune should he divorce her, was simply sent to sea for about nine months of every year in order to get her out of the way. On the *QE2*, she was able to indulge her tense and intense self to her heart's content, and it was only during the American school holidays, when her children were flown out to join her for a few weeks, that her snivelling temporarily stopped.

Mrs Q had a soft spot for officers, but over the nine years she spent on the ship, as she aged and lost what precious little had remained of her looks and her hair, the rank of the officer on whose arm she swanned into the public rooms slowly fell. In her first year on board she hooked up with a suitably senior officer; by her last year she was shagging the telecommunications officer, a man widely known for his powerfully unpleasant body odour.

Another regular passenger who had a longlived affair with a ship's officer was a modern siren who started life as plain old Sandra Jarvis-Daly, the daughter of a hotel waitress. All that changed when she converted to Islam, changed her name to Soraya and married small, portly and polite billionaire, Turkish-Saudi Arabian arms dealer 'Mr Fixit' Adnan Khashoggi.

And it changed again, thirteen years and five children later, when she won one of the largest divorce settlements in history, according to the 1992 *Guinness Book of Records* – reports vary from £2 million, an unimaginable fortune in those days, to an unbelievable £540 million.

Described by the late English portrait and fashion photographer Norman Parkinson CBE, whose comparisons included the likes of gorgeous Texan model Jerry Hall, as 'one of the most naturally beautiful women' he had ever snapped, Soraya had the world at her feet at the very peak of her sexual power in the 1980s, when she was a *QE2* regular. As the wife of one of the wealthiest men in the world, Soraya flitted between three London homes, another in New York, two Swiss apartments and a mansion in Marbella; she had a horse-racing stud and at least five cars, including a Rolls Royce and a Maserati, plus private planes and luxury yachts. Not only was her financial pull astonishingly strong, but her sexual allure was so irresistible that she could look a man into bed, it was said, with a flick of her hair and a flash of her eyes.

Clearly.

Soraya eventually had nine children. One of these, Petrina, now in her 30s, thought she saw an uncanny physical resemblance between herself and two of her close friends, twins Alexandra and Victoria Aitken. Their father is Jonathan, a UK Tory cabinet minister who served time in prison for perjury – and DNA testing proved that Jonathan was, in fact, Petrina's father.

Soraya was a passenger on the *QE2* during her pregnancy with Petrina (and when she was still married to Adnan), and there were many who wondered whether the baby might not be the offspring of one of the ship's senior officers. His and Soraya's affair did, after all, last for some years, even if it was on and off. (Soraya also had an affair with Winston Churchill's grandson, also called Winston – a liaison that ended his marriage.)

The lives of the rich and famous are every bit as tacky, when it comes down to it, as anything you might see on *Jerry Springer*. UK movie director Guy Ritchie (with whom Petrina was at one time romantically linked), for instance, won a reported £50-million divorce settlement from his obscenely wealthy wife, Madonna, amid rumours of her affair with an American basketball star. Jerry Hall discovered her husband, rock-star Mick, had fathered a child out of wedlock and took him for a cool $15-20 million, nailing him for both the humiliation of having to put up with his inescapably public infidelity and the relatively thankless job of raising his kids while he was 'on the road' (and all that came with that).

Soraya, for her part, remained discreet to the end. Her record-setting divorce from Adnan notwithstanding, the two remained friends – perhaps not least for, ultimately, the acknowledgement by both of infidelity during their marriage. In 1987, for Christmas, Adnan presented her with a ruby necklace. His new wife, Lamia, got one too – but hers was bigger.

Now in her 60s, Soraya lives quietly in the UK and works as a florist. Some years ago, some of her journals and photograph albums ended up in a junkshop and became the locus of a blackmail attempt. As in any personal account there were, sure, details of an intimate nature. But more moving were the entries that revealed Soraya, once the pampered consort of one of the richest men on earth, and a woman so blindingly beautiful that men willingly derailed their lives for her, to be a somewhat lonely and very ordinary divorcee: 'Took the children to Regent's Park Zoo. Tried to collect my prescription and glasses (both places closed).'

§

Officers weren't the only crew who were joined by family: after a staff member had worked aboard for a year, they were entitled to invite a family member for a free six-week stint at sea. My mother, Greta, whom everyone now calls 'Granny' (she's in her 70s, although she was an elegant lady in her 50s when she joined me on the *QE2* in my fourth year of cruising), was so excited about her forthcoming trip that she neglected to tell her travel agent that not only did she require a return South Africa/United Kingdom flight, but that she would be picking up the ship in the UK to go to the States – and so she arrived in the UK, after months of careful planning, without an American visa.

Greta's trip was, in fact, dogged by problems from the start. Before we discovered the calamity of the missing visa, we'd already had one near-cancellation, when Steiner unexpectedly declined to renew my contract at the beginning of that fourth year. This cavalier treatment of staff wasn't unusual, especially when it came to the role of assistant manager or manager of the salon, positions that were much vied-for, for their wealth of privileges on board.

I was in Port Elizabeth at the time – Greta had been too nervous to fly to the UK by herself, so I'd taken leave at the end of my contract (fully expecting it to be renewed the following year) to fly home and accompany her back to the UK. I phoned and pleaded my case to Steiner, who had already given my assistant-manager job to someone else, stressing that my mother was planning to join me, and they kindly agreed to re-employ me as a 'consultant', with all privileges intact.

And, at the eleventh hour – more specifically, five minutes before the ship was due to leave Southampton – the *QE2*'s purser came through for us: he paid a sizeable fine and did a bit of sweet-talking, and Greta was given a crew visa for the States.

By then poor Greta thought she'd never get on board, and by the time she did, she was very stressed. Thinking to give her an exciting send-off and restore her faith in cruising, I took her up to the enclosed outer deck where you could sit on deckchairs and watch the land recede as the ship pulled away from the dock. She was almost calm again, comfortably ensconced in a deck chair, when the engines started, their rumbling thrumming and throbbing reverberating through the ship's superstructure. Greta's eyes flew open in alarm, and when the ship began moving away from the harbour, she made her decision. Standing up, she said to me, 'I want to get off. And I want to get off *now*.'

I laughed. 'Tough shit,' I said. 'You're on. And you're going to stay on.'

Greta's first night didn't put any of her fears to rest, either. The seas were quite rough and Greta was woken in the small hours by the sound of her telephone falling from the side table. Panicked, she picked it up, reconnected it, and phoned me. Unbeknown to her, my phone too had been knocked off the hook by the turbulent conditions, and she couldn't raise me.

Now seriously worried, Greta opened her door and poked her head out. She looked up and down the corridor. It was late and nobody was about.

The next morning, when I went to fetch her for breakfast, I found a seriously frightened woman. 'I thought everyone had abandoned ship and left me behind!' she whimpered. Then she packed her bags and, without further ado, left her luxurious stateroom and moved down to my staff cabin, where she slept happily in the spare bed for the remainder of the voyage.

Despite these rocky beginnings, it didn't take Greta long to get used to the luxurious life on board a cruise liner. It helped that visiting family members were treated with special attention – free salon treatments, for instance, and the best tables in the restaurants. It was clear, too, that Greta's friends had rallied round before her departure and helped fit her out with jewellery and a range of beautiful formal outfits; these, combined with her daily 5pm hair appointment and her 5.30 makeup, manicure and pedicure, made sure she always looked like a movie star. There was little that could make her giggle more like a girl than when a crew member greeted us by exclaiming, 'How nice, Richard! You've brought your sister on board!'

Greta, who was born in the one-horse town of Cradock shortly after the Second World War ended and the Depression hadn't yet lifted, took to the high life as if to the manor born. My own salon clients on board were excited to have Greta there, and pulled out all the stops to show her a good time, taking her with them on their limousine rides to the finest restaurants in the glittering capitals of the world.

One of these invitations was to have breakfast in the famous Oak Room at New York's Ritz Hotel, and I went along too. As we rounded a corner in the hotel, Greta collided with a diminutive black woman. This was in the 1980s and Greta, like many South Africans of her age, was an unapologetic racist. While the two women collected themselves and Greta prepared herself to be outraged, the black woman said, very politely, 'Oh, I'm so sorry!'

Greta was charmed, and after our two parties had gone our separate ways, whispered to me, 'But she looked very familiar.'

'That's because she's Whoopi Goldberg,' I said.

Greta went pink with pleasure. Whoopi Goldberg! A famous movie star! As far as Greta was concerned, Whoopi could have purposely elbowed her in the ribs, and that would have been okay.

Greta loved royalty almost as much as she loved movie stars, so another highlight of her trip was meeting and shaking the hand of both Prince Edward, a passenger for part of that cruise (it was, coincidentally, the first time he'd ever been on board), and photographer-to-the-stars and (more importantly for Greta) first-cousin-once-removed-to-the-Queen Lord Lichfield, who took the time to sit and chat with her.

The presence on board of these – and other – royal personages wasn't unusual: the Royal Family tended to use the *QE2* as something of an extension to their own official yacht, the *Britannia*. (The *Britannia*, like the *QE2*, has been decommissioned; during its lifetime it sailed over a million miles, calling at 600 ports in 135 countries; it has been moored at the Edinburgh Port of Leith since 1997 and is open to the public.) In 1990 the Queen and the Duke of Edinburgh transferred from the *Britannia* to the *QE2* by Royal Barge, and the Queen became the first reigning monarch to sail on a commercial line with passengers.

I met many members of the Royal Family, from the Queen Mum and Princesses Anne and Margaret, down to some of the 'lesser' royals, during my time on the *QE2*, when we were often required to do cruise-pasts of the *Britannia*. People often ask me if I'd met Princess Diana, and if so, what I thought of her.

I did meet her, and I didn't think much. To be fair to Di, the circumstances were shambolic: it was in 1987, and she'd come on board to host what was then one of the largest children's parties afloat, with 500 Southampton school kids running riot all over the place, like mice let out of paper bags. The ship had sailed with the children to the Isle of Wight, which is where we picked up Princess Di – she'd been helicoptered there, and was transferred to the *QE2* by barge in the pouring rain.

Di was damp and bedraggled and, ahead of the formalities and festivities, which were to be attended by the press and any number of other hangers-on, needed a quick fixer-up. One of the *QE2*'s senior staff came into the salon and instructed me to 'fit her in'.

I paused in what I was doing and said to him, 'You must be kidding. Look around.' The salon was heaving – every chair was full, every dryer was in use, every stylist was working their fingers to the bone, and there were people queuing out the door.

'She's the Princess of Wales,' he hissed. 'Fit. Her. In.'

I was still muttering under my breath when a small commotion followed by a strange silence changed the atmosphere in the salon: the Princess had arrived. She was surrounded by a security detail and as many people as could get close to her. Giving me a quick, apologetic smile, she slipped into the seat I had, somewhat grumpily, vacated for her. Perhaps she was aware of the inconvenience she'd caused; maybe my thin-lipped irritation was obvious; or it could just have been her natural shyness: whatever the reason, she sat quietly and a little nervously, her hands clutched together in her lap, while I dried and styled her hair. We didn't exchange a single word.

One of my mom Greta's proudest moments in my career came several years later when I was almost made hairdresser to the Queen. It came about in a curiously low-key way, with a Steiner bigwig coming on board and showing me a diagram of a hair set. 'Would you be able to follow this?' he asked. I looked at it and said yes – it was a very simple style. 'Good,' he said, 'because Queen Elizabeth's hairdresser is about to retire and we're looking for a new one.'

My name was put forward but this was at a time when 'buying British' had become a national obsession and even Princess Di was under fire for having a Mercedes Benz when a Rover would have done just as well. So I, a South African, lost the job of Hair to the Throne to one of Steiner's senior hairstylists, Ian Carmichael.

Ian, a Scotsman, was known for his outrageous behaviour in the *QE2*'s public rooms. One of his party tricks was to casually sling a leg up over his partner's shoulder while dancing. And he didn't confine his acrobatics to shipboard. Once, at the end of the charter in Osaka in Japan, Ian went ashore with a group of hairdressers for a celebratory night out. They got completely plastered and, returning to the dock, decided to show Osaka what they were all about: they would, they decided, do a 'Fame' dance, using the cars parked up and down the harbour as a stage set.

For anyone who doesn't remember the movie *Fame*, which came out in 1980, and followed a group of students through their studies at the New York High School of Performing Arts, there's a dance sequence in it, to the Irene Cara song 'Fame', in which the lithe and athletic students dance on cars parked in the street.

Alas for Ian and his cohorts: if they were lithe when in a sober state, drunk, they were like a troupe of baby elephants. Much damage was done to the vehicles they cavorted across, including broken windscreen wipers and rearview mirrors, dented bonnets and fenders, and the like. There was, of course, hell to pay for it the next morning – and, as far as I remember, Ian had to fork out a fairly substantial sum in damages.

Ian, whose cheek was legendary, came close to being eviscerated one evening during a crew party, an occasion when one of the public rooms was opened to all the crew including the roughty-toughty 'backroom boys' such as the staff from the engine rooms and the deckhands – men who didn't take kindly to homosexuals. Ian, blissfully unaware (or just stirring shit), took this opportunity to sashay into the men's room, where several of these 'real' men were relieving themselves, swinging a keychain at the end of which winked a figurine of Dorothy from *The Wizard of Oz*, and enquire archly, 'Are any of you lads friends of this wee lassie?' It's unlikely many of his audience understood the exact meaning of the question but Ian's intention was clear, and it required some very nifty footwork to get him out of there in one piece.

(That wasn't the only time the queens on board played with their lives in pursuit of flirtation. Another was after the ship's refit in Germany, when it sailed across the North Sea to Southampton, and the SAS took the opportunity to use it for manoeuvres, practising ocean jumps from helicopters and other sea-type military drills. It was an incomparable thrill for the ship's shirt-lifters to suddenly be inundated by thirty super-fit SAS paratroopers, all built like Adonis. One very girly waiter who, in Ian Carmichael style, went too far when he propositioned one, paid for this outrage when the paratrooper grasped him round the throat with one hand and lifted him bodily off the deck, allowing him to dangle there, feet kicking feebly, for some time while he reconsidered his suggestion.)

When Ian was hired by Bond girl Olga Kurylenko, who starred in *Quantum of Solace* in 2008, to do her hair for red-carpet appearances, I was amused to read that he admitted that Olga and the Queen opt for 'very different hairstyles'.

'Queen Elizabeth has always gone for the traditional look, one that's easy for her to maintain; it's her look and she is happy with it,' he told reporters. Then he showed a flash of his former flamboyance when he added, 'It's been a case of my work going from "By Appointment To The Queen" to "On Her Majesty's Secret Service"!'

I often think about that hair-set diagram I was shown when I see the Queen making public appearances on television today: from that day to this, not a thing about her hairstyle has changed; Ian is evidently still following that diagram.

As for my mother: she was bitterly disappointed that I'd missed out on my opportunity to become part of the Royal entourage – particularly since she'd already started bragging to her friends about it.

10. The Infirmary

The *QE2* boasted a fully equipped infirmary and operating theatre, staffed by two doctors, four professional nurses, a chemist and a dentist, among other medical specialists. While they were frequented, of course, by the ship's passengers, the infirmary did double-time for the crew whenever the ship left a port known for its exotic attractions – Rio de Janeiro and Thailand being two of them. After one of these landfalls, the daily crew surgery, held from 8am to 10am, was all a-gogo – and penicillin was the medication of necessity.

Once, when we were docked in Pusan, in Korea, two of the night engineers (who therefore got day shore leave) and I decided to step out and see what the town had to offer. We'd heard about a military tattoo-type drill that was held in an arena in a nearby town, and that's where we wanted to go.

By the time we'd got to land and changed money, however, we discovered that the buses that ran to the next town left every hour, and we'd missed the previous one by five minutes. So, with an hour to kill at 8 in the morning, we did what any self-respecting tourists would do: we found a bar.

It was called The Hollywood Bar, and was run by an elderly gent (who sat at the door, issuing instructions by clicking his fingers) and an elderly woman who invited us to call her Mama-san. We ordered three rum-and-Cokes, and made ourselves comfortable at the bar. The old guy clicked his fingers three times, and from behind a beaded curtain emerged three beautiful young Korean women. We were, surprise surprise, in a brothel.

Quickly the three drinks became six – it turned out we were buying for the girls, too – and six became twelve, and just about as quickly, our money ran out. By this stage, one of the night engineers had negotiated a price with the girls, so I was sent back to the ship to get more bucks.

(In my defence, I did repeatedly try to fend off 'my' girl, who told me her name was Tiger Lily. 'I've got a headache,' I said – hey, it's an excuse that's worked for millions of unwilling wives! – but all she did was smile sweetly and begin massaging my shoulders in a really rather pleasant way. And when one of the engineers said to her, 'You might as well give up with Japie – he's a moffie,' she just lowered her eyes and giggled.)

By the time I got back to The Hollywood Bar, yet another night engineer, Vince, had joined the merry throng. He was also keen to be in on the action, but declared himself bankrupt. For reasons we didn't understand – except, perhaps, we'd been so thoroughly ripped off already that throwing in a freebie wouldn't hurt – Vince got himself a girl for nothing.

So we didn't get to see the military drill in the nearby town, but I did see some things that day that impressed me. Tiger Lily turned out to be an astoundingly supple and athletic performer. To add to the bizarreness of the morning, the hotel we all washed up at – the price we'd negotiated included the cost of the rooms – had a phone system that linked all the rooms, so the night engineers and I called each other from time to time to compare experiences.

It was a few days later, when we were back at sea and I wandered past the queue outside the infirmary during crew-surgery hours, that I realised that Vince had been given not one free gift during our shore leave, but two: there he was, squirming with discomfort, lined up with the rest of the boys, waiting for his penicillin shot.

§

Excellent as the medical care on board was, the infirmary did let me down once. It was during the time of the Tokyo/Osaka charter, when we were more or less permanently moored for six months. I was irritated to be stuck in Japan, not least because my twin nephews, Jason and Brandon, had just been born, and when I put in for leave to be allowed to go home and see them, it was refused.

So my mood wasn't improved at all when I woke up one morning with very red, scratchy eyes. I was working as a bar cashier in the Mauretania restaurant during this time, and to save clients having to look at my unsightly peepers, I put on a pair of sunglasses before reporting for duty.

One of the managers was a woman we called Frau Rottweiler. Her raison d'être was to find someone less than alert on duty, and her personal signature was sneaking quietly into a public room, sidling up to the bar cashier (who, not being allowed to do anything constructive to fill dead time, was often dozing with his/her eyes open), and bang loudly on the side of the till. The obvious thrill she got from this was deeply annoying.

Frau Rottweiler came stalking into the Mauretania, intent on catching me doing something I shouldn't, or not doing something I should, and her face lit up with evil pleasure when she saw me.

'Take those sunglasses off immediately!' she snapped. 'You know they're not part of regulation dress.'

'There's something wrong with my eyes,' I told her.

She sniffed. 'You shouldn't have partied so hard last night. Take them off!'

I did and was rewarded when Frau Rottweiler did a double-take. 'Jesus!' she said. 'Put them on again, quickly! Put them on! And report to the infirmary. Go, go!'

There was only a nurse on duty that morning, but she wasn't fazed by the state of my eyes. She told me there was some conjunctivitis going around and gave me a tube of ointment. 'Squeeze a pea-sized drop under each eyelid now, and again tonight, and tomorrow you'll be right as rain,' she said confidently.

The next morning my eyes were one hundred percent worse. Bright red and slightly swollen, they were also starting to ooze a thin yellow pus. I returned to the infirmary and spoke to the doctor on duty. He was similarly unconcerned but did prescribe some stronger eyedrops. 'You'll be fine by tomorrow,' he said.

The next morning I literally couldn't open my eyes. I groped my way to the basin and splashed warm water on my face until the pus, which had set to a glue-like state and jammed my eyelashes together, had softened enough for me to ease my peepers open. Then even I did a double-take: my lids were swollen, the irises were an angry red, and my eyes were oozing freely.

Seized with anxiety, I groped my way back to the doctor. He nodded sagely and told me it was a pretty severe case of conjunctivitis, but to carry on with the eyedrops and be patient. 'It'll get better over the next few days,' he assured me.

Instead, it got steadily worse. Two days later my eyes were swollen shut and even when I could force them open into slits, I couldn't see – a thin white film had formed over the surface of my eyeball, obscuring my vision.

By the end of that week, I'd been to the infirmary twice every day, to have iodine squeezed into my eyes. The doctor, more concerned now, had examined my corneas through a magnifying glass, muttering and shaking his head. He could see no damage there, he said, but he also was at a loss as to why my eyes weren't getting better.

At the beginning of the second week, the doctor decided I needed to see an eye specialist. The ship's agent – usually a local, land-based person who was the go-between for logistical arrangements such as supplies and staff to be brought on board – was summoned to fetch me. He led me down the gangway and helped me into a waiting taxi, and we sped off to a hospital that specialised in the treatment of eyes.

The ship's agent and the doctor spoke no English; I spoke no Japanese. In addition, the doctor was apparently having a bad day, as he was ill-tempered and rough. Forcing open each of my eyes in turn, he snatched up what looked like a glass swizzle stick, which he used to scrape mercilessly at the white film that had formed over the cornea. The pain was excruciating. When it was over, I was handed six bottles, three with pink lids and three with blue. Using impatient and obscure sign language, the doctor instructed me on the use of these fluids and sent me on my way.

Two weeks later the bottles of fluid were finished and my eyes were no better. By now I was effectively blind: I wore sunglasses permanently and groped my way around the ship. I was useless to the staff and miserable as sin. I sent word to the Steiner head office telling them I wanted to go back to South Africa and get proper treatment. In reality, I had more or less given up on ever having healthy eyes again; I actually just wanted to go home to my mother and get some genuine TLC.

I got a telex from Steiner instructing me to fly to London instead. When I phoned to speak to Clive Warshaw, the big boss, I was given a thorough drubbing. 'You applied for leave four weeks ago and it was turned down, and now suddenly you're sick enough to go home? What rubbish!' he barked. 'I've never heard of anyone being disembarked for conjunctivitis. If it's really as bad as you say, we'll arrange an eye surgeon to look at you here in London.' And he disconnected the call.

The flight to London was a seemingly neverending, frightening blur. The ship's agent dropped me off at Tokyo airport and drove off, leaving me alone and sightless. The flight stopped twice, in Bangkok and Frankfurt, and both times I had to change planes. At Heathrow, I groped my way miserably through passport control, collected my baggage – by describing it to someone standing with me at the carousel – and was helped by a kind stranger to the Tube station. From there, I travelled to the other side of London. Exhausted and weepy, in deep discomfort, I made my way blindly along pavements and across streets to the Steiner headquarters, where Clive was waiting for me.

And finally – finally! – the penny dropped. I took off my sunglasses and Clive paled. 'Oh my god!' he said. 'I'm so sorry! I didn't realise!'

From that moment, everything went more smoothly. Clive organised a car to take me back to Heathrow. He booked me onto a Business Class seat and arranged for help for me with boarding and getting off in Cape Town.

There, my mother was waiting to take me straight to an eye specialist, who sat me down in his chair, examined me thoroughly, and said, 'I know what the problem is.' I'd heard this before, so I wasn't convinced, but this time the diagnosis was correct: the very first ointment that the nurse had prescribed to treat the initial conjunctivitis had caused an allergic reaction in my eyes, which, left untreated, had simply got worse and worse as time passed.

One of the things the doctor had to do was remove the white film that had reformed over my cornea, much as the forceful Japanese doctor had. For this, I was required to sit in a chair, with my head clamped into a machine and my chin resting on a support, so that he could scrape the film away – which he did with a scalpel and, mercifully, infinite gentleness.

And suddenly, for the first time in three weeks, I could see! I sat there, head clamped, darting my eyes around at all I'd been missing. And a little metal tab secured to the side of the machine attracted my attention. I looked sideways, squinting to get it into focus, and when I read what was stamped there, I had to laugh: 'Made in Japan'. I'd travelled halfway across the world to be put to rights with the help of a machine made in the country I'd started in.

That all ended well: I was granted six weeks' recuperative leave, and I spent the whole time in Port Elizabeth with my brother and new nephews.

§

For elderly or unfit passengers thinking of having a heart attack, there was no place to do it like the *QE2* – in such a contained environment, and with specialist medical staff on board, you were assured of quick treatment by the right people.

Unfortunately, heart attacks among our elderly clients weren't that unusual, and the staff code for such an eventuality was 'Starlight, starlight, starlight.' So if you heard the captain announcing over the tannoy system, 'Starlight, starlight, starlight: 4 Deck, G Stairway,' you knew that the medical staff on duty were springing into action. These highly trained personnel were able, in this kind of emergency, to reach the stricken passenger, regardless of his or her location on the ship, in under three minutes.

The code for flooding was 'Niagara, Niagara, Niagara.' (Obviously, this was flooding of a modest kind, like a toilet overflowing, and not something serious like being holed by an iceberg – in which case I suppose the code would have been 'Abandon ship! Abandon ship! Abandon ship!') At one stage we had on board a very outspoken and rather gorgeous woman called Lynette, an assistant manager. Whenever Lynette walked past an attractive male, she would announce to any crew present, 'Niagara, Niagara, Niagara.' Of course, their response would always be, 'Careful, Lynette, don't have a starlight, starlight, starlight.'

§

While excellent medical care and prescription drugs were available from the infirmary for those who needed them, recreational drugs were also freely on tap on the ship. This I discovered on an early cruise when Robert Ellis, a 'businessman' whose business just happened to be carrying large quantities of cocaine between Colombia and England, asked me to buy some 'cut', or diluent, for him during a stopover in New York.

Rob had come into the salon for a haircut and took to me. A few days later, while I was giving him a trim, he asked me *sotto voce* if I knew where to get some 'real dope'. 'All I've been able to get on this ship is shitty hashish,' he said.

As it happened, I had a bankie of good South African dagga I'd picked up in Cape Town a few weeks before. I told Rob this and he could hardly contain his excitement. 'Skin me up a joint – no tobacco,' he said. 'Meet me on 1 Deck at 7pm.'

This I duly did and, along with Sheena, a Californian massage therapist and all-round party girl, we smoked the joint with Rob. Once it was finished Rob turned to me with a dreamy look in his eyes. 'Thanks, guy,' he said. 'Have this for your troubles.' He handed me a small envelope.

As a young South African in the '80s, I had been exposed to very few 'designer' drugs: cocaine, for instance, was still the recreational substance of choice for mainly the select few in high-stress 'glamorous' occupations like acting, modelling and advertising; and although ecstasy had begun to make its mark on the club scene, it wasn't easily obtainable.

What Rob gave me looked like speed, and I didn't want any part of it. A few weeks previously I'd snorted some speed at a crew party and hadn't been able to sleep for three days. But Sheena, who was more experienced than me, looked at it closely and said, 'This is pure cocaine!'

I still wasn't sure, so Sheena chopped out a modest line for me and a monster one for herself. It was the first time I'd snorted coke and I took to it like the proverbial duck. I still remember the feeling it gave me: I walked back down to my cabin thinking, *I Am The Greatest!*

So when Rob asked me to buy cut for him for his coke, I agreed. I wasn't sure how to go about it but I was a resourceful young man and, after some discreet asking around, discovered that you could buy any number of drugs, both legal and otherwise, on 42nd Street in Manhattan. This was hardly surprising – before the clean-up of the Times Square area in the late 1990s, this major crosstown street was known for its grindhouse theatres which showed mainly exploitation movies (including graphically gory horror flicks, slasher films and 'shockumentaries' that focused on taboo subjects like torture, rape, bestiality and incest), its brothels and peep shows. Its clientele was every bit as dodgy – pimps and prostitutes, petty gangsters and rough thrill-seekers of every colour, creed and sexual orientation.

Part of this subculture was the availability – if you knew were to look – of any number of illegal drugs. But there were also serried ranks of drugstores selling legal drug-related paraphernalia – not only the papers and pipes associated with marijuana, but also medicines like Lidocaine, a general anaesthetic often used in dental surgery.

Lidocaine was (and is) often used as a diluent for cocaine. It's popular not only because, in powder form, it's practically identical in appearance to cocaine, but the fact that it numbs the gums (as does cocaine) gives users the impression that they're the fortunate recipients of high-quality coke, when in fact they're using a diluted product.

So it was off to 42nd Street for me, and there, using money Rob had given me, I bought a large quantity of Lidocaine. (Interestingly enough, at the time the Lidocaine cost almost as much as the pure cocaine, so Rob's reasons for cutting his product eluded me.) In return, Rob gave me a full film canister of pure cocaine.

This opened my eyes to the thriving drug trade on board the ship. There were at least six merchants of various kinds at any time in the crew who sold mainly cocaine and marijuana (which at some stage some of the more ambitious ones began cutting with heroin, which put me off buying from them); and poppers (amyl nitrite) was also popular. Dagga was, in fact, available in such abundance in many seaports that it was given away free if you bought a quantity of cocaine. The waiters, in particular, were cokeheads, but not particularly keen on dagga, and they often passed the marijuana on to me.

But cocaine, too, was in abundant supply: once, in Colombia, I watched as a dealer chopped a rock of coke off a rugby-ball-sized lump of it. Sometimes there was so much of it on board that instead of chopping lines, we'd chop out our initials in coke before snorting it. A scurrilous *News of the World* report around that time dubbed the *QE2* 'The Cocaine Cruiser' – something the higher-ups were very quick to flatly deny.

It obviously wasn't a good idea to have drugs of any kind anywhere on you or even in your cabin when the ship went into port, particularly since it was normal practice in some places for the customs guys to come on board with sniffer dogs – in Los Angeles in 1988, for instance, we were delayed for six hours while US Customs subjected the ship, the crew, the passengers and all the luggage to a dog-search. So we got clever at finding hiding places throughout the ship for our stashes – behind pictures in the public corridors was one favourite, and in the fire dampers in some of the removable ceiling slabs was another.

Years after I left the *QE2*, the ship was in port in Cape Town, where I had returned to live, and I got a special pass to take my friend Axel aboard to show him where I'd spent so many years of my life. Passing through one of the fire doors, I said to Axel, 'We used to hide our dope stash up here when we went into a harbour,' and I casually ran my hand along the ledge on top – and came away with a big brick of prize hashish! So this tradition was clearly still very much alive.

§

The crew parties on the *QE2* were legendary, and, particularly around year-end, could go on for days, a movable feast in a different venue each evening. These were sanctioned by the officers – it was a way of getting at least some of the thousand-plus staff together to let their hair down. They started late – around 11pm – and often ended the next morning. There was one unwritten rule, though: no matter how dreadful you might be feeling the morning after, it wasn't an excuse not to report for duty.

So the crew partied hard – but we also worked our butts off, and sometimes it was necessary, after a heavy night's jolling, to get help through the long working day that followed. Here, 42nd Street helped too, in particular the GNC (Greater Nutrition Center), ostensibly a health shop but for us a warehouse of floor-to-ceiling pick-me-ups. Favourites were Diet Pep and Dexatrim, both supposedly all-natural fat-burning products, one hit of which would give instant lift-off.

When those weren't available for some reason, we'd raid the Steiner supply cupboards for 'Royal Jelly' tonic ampoules – eight of these swallowed straight down as the salon opened would be enough to get us through to lunchtime.

I did, however, have one client who wouldn't let me touch her hair unless I had a hangover – she believed that I styled better in that slightly altered state. Her name was Beverley and she was a singer with the Mick Urry Orchestra, one of the two big bands resident on the ship at the time. She'd book the first appointment of the day, knowing we wouldn't be too busy then, and come in with a questioning look in her eyes. 'Are you hungover?' she'd ask. If I said yes, she'd sit down and we'd proceed. If it was no, she'd say, 'I'll come back tomorrow, then.'

She was among the first to call me 'Dick', a name I didn't much like – although it beat 'Japie'.

Of course, drug escapades weren't confined to shipboard. There were several ports that caused an excited buzz among the crew, and Pattaya in Thailand was chief among them. This coastal city with its beaches and other tourist attractions, and wild, wild nightlife, never failed to raise expectations: as we neared Thailand, the staff would start getting antsy – they wanted to *party*!

In Pattaya, you were sure to be picked up – either by prostitutes or by the police. Licentiousness and corruption were as rife as each other, and if you weren't paying a transsexual to give you the best blowjob of your life (and, if you were me, to lift your favourite gold lighter out of your pocket while s/he was about it), you were paying off the police to get yourself or your buddies out of jail. The only differential was the time: if it was before 10pm you were probably being propositioned by a whore ('I'm from Hong Kong; I've got a hotel room' – a favourite pickup line from sex workers keen to separate themselves from the local 'rough trade'); after 10pm and it was the police who were asking you to cross their palms with silver in return for your freedom.

The BBC travel documentary programme *Whicker's World* was filming in Pattaya when we were there on a world cruise. Presenter Alan Whicker described the place as 'the new Havana' and said it was 'where every sailor dreams of coming to rest and relax'. If the reports were to be believed, many husbands dreamed of the same thing: apparently, after the show aired in the UK, there were marital squabbles aplenty and even some acrimonious divorces, when wives who'd waited faithfully back home for their shipboard-employed significant others saw them dallying with the Pattaya lovelies.

On a more sinister note, a *QE2* steward called Steve Wright was on that shore leave, and he was captured on camera by Alan Whicker's cameras, kissing a prostitute. The twice-married, twice-divorced father of two was later sentenced to life in prison for murdering five women in the UK – all prostitutes. Steve admitted at his trial that he'd begun frequenting prostitutes while working on the *QE2*: 'There was a young crew and it was quite normal,' he said.

Steve – who became known as 'the Suffolk Strangler' and was apprehended after the largest manhunt in the history of the Suffolk constabulary – was hardly noticed on the ship. He would hang around our social gatherings, always on the outskirts and never contributing much, and while I can't say he was actively lecherous, there was perhaps something strangely needy about him that made everyone a bit uneasy. A waiter at the time, quoted later in a newspaper article, remembered, 'Steve would sniff around all the girls and particularly the beauticians.'

Newspaper reports at the time of his conviction in 2008 carried statements from his ex wife, Diane Cole (who also worked on the ship, as a sales assistant), about his interest in a Steiner beautician, Suzy Lamplugh, who disappeared in 1986 and was never found.

If sex wasn't your thing, there was shopping to do in Pattaya – and *how*! This was a place where you could first select the garment of your liking (shirt, suit, gown, whatever took your fancy) and then choose from a range of designer labels that would, while you waited, be sewn into it. Why bother to pay directly through the nose for a Gucci or Versace when a knockoff that couldn't be told from the original by anybody you'd be associating with in normal life – *and bore the stamp of the designer* – was available for a fraction of the cost? Louis Vuitton luggage, every bit as stylish as Mr Vuitton's, was to be had for what you'd spend on a T-shirt back home. It was retail-therapy heaven.

Thailand, along with Laos and Myanmar, borders the 'Golden Triangle', one of the world's hotspots for narcotics production – and this country, like much of Southeast Asia, has draconian penalties for drug possession: the death sentence, for instance, if you're caught trafficking heroin, and life imprisonment for being caught with a range of other mind-altering substances. Yet, perversely, the drug trade here is rife and usage very widespread.

A group of about eight of us from the *QE2* contributed in our small way to this nefarious underworld by, on our arrival in

Pattaya, hiring a modest convoy of Jeeps and motorcycles (which, incidentally, are to be had for more or less the price of a pack of smokes, and nobody asks if you're licensed to drive) and heading off up the Khao Phra Tam Nak, a hill that offers a panoramic view of the city and is topped by the Wat Khao Phra Bat, an eighteen-metre-tall Buddha statue. What better place, I ask, to smoke a big fat joint?

The road up (and, of course, back) is a winding and somewhat perilous one, but we got there, and, in the shadow of the Buddha, lit up.

Some time later we decided to head back down into the city and partake of whatever nightlife was on offer, and accordingly remounted our bikes and Jeeps. I was behind one of the Jeeps, riding pillion on a 150cc Scrambler with my friend Krish, when the driver of the Jeep suddenly realised he was going too fast to negotiate a corner and hit the brakes. The Jeep spun spectacularly, three times, but by some miracle didn't plunge down the hillside.

Once the dust and confusion had settled, I said to the driver of the Jeep, 'Where's the guy who was holding on to the rollbar?'

'Which guy?' he asked.

'The guy,' I said, '*the guy.*' I had smoked a big fat joint, remember, so my speech centre was a bit disconnected; and even as I was asking about him, I was wondering if my seeing some dude cartwheel into the air above our heads and disappear from view had been merely a by-product of the dagga.

We all looked around, shambolic and stoned. Then some bright spark had the notion that the guy may have gone over the edge of the hill. We trooped to the side of the road and peered down – and there, lying in a ravine, being ravenously licked by an excited pack of feral puppies, was the missing man.

It took what seemed a tremendously long time for three of us to scramble down the hill, shoo the dogs away, rouse the unconscious man (who said, not surprisingly, that he had a headache), and half-drag him back up to the road. There, we bundled him back into the Jeep and hightailed it down the hill, back to port. We were lucky to find a launch waiting, and we piled the concussed individual on board with strict instructions to the launch operator to take him straight to the ship's doctor when he got him back to the boat. (He wasn't, apparently, seriously injured, although he did hold his head at an odd angle for the rest of the cruise. And, like Brian, he never went out with us again either.)

That done, we turned around and headed straight back up Khao Phra Tam Nak hill – for a top-up of THC. This wasn't, you understand, for reasons of pure hedonism: 'I need a joint to calm my nerves,' the Jeep driver told us as we stood around watching the launch carrying the accident victim pull out to sea. And we all agreed that was in order.

So there we were, in the shadow of the Wat Khao Phra Bat buddha for the second time that night, skinning up, when suddenly we found ourselves in the middle of a brain-frying, stomach-churning, heart-palpitating *Midnight Express*-type scenario: there were Thai police everywhere, with guns and spotlights and a lot of unintelligible screaming. The police were shouting a lot too.

Krish had the only marijuana – a small matchbox-full – which he palmed to me. I put it in my pocket. Another in our party, a guy called Paul, was caught in the act of trying to conceal a brick-sized block of hashish; Paul panicked and, with the hashish clutched tightly in his hand, headed off on foot down the ravine (unbeknown to Paul, or any of us, the Buddha statue is safely enclosed in a fenced reserve: there was nowhere for Paul to run).

But Paul was, for the meantime, safe: the Thai police had eyes only for Krish and me, who had mounted the Scrambler with the notion of making a run for it. They trained their guns on us and, with the certain knowledge that I was going to die in a Thai prison, I somehow managed to extract the matchbox of dagga from my pocket and drop it at my feet. There followed ten minutes of pure hysteria: the police screaming at us and patting us down; Krish and me screaming back, protesting our innocence and our foreignness (which of course made us even more of a target: foreigner drug users are not looked on kindly by the Thai government).

And then: 'You can go,' said the dude who seemed to be in charge. He was sulky about it: he *knew* we had drugs on us, and he was mightily annoyed he couldn't find them.

I was so buoyed by this sudden capitulation, and so stupidly stoned, that as Krish and I got on the bike, I actually bent down, scratched around at my feet, found the matchbox, and put it back in my pocket. And the next minute we were flying down the hill, the wind in our faces and blissful freedom beckoning.

At the gate of the reserve (which we noticed then, for the first time: yes, the hill *is* fenced), we joined the rest of our mates and waited for Paul… who came trotting down the road towards us, holding the hashish brick which he had, insanely, held on to, up high, a victorious grin on his face… which was supplanted by terror as the cops came down behind him, spotlights at full flood, and caught him in the act *again*. Paul, too stoned to notice a brisk wind blowing, turned and chucked the brick up like a frisbee, intending for it to be lost in the undergrowth somewhere beyond the searching eye of the lights – but it blew directly back at him and landed, with horrible obviousness, right at his feet.

So, finally, we *were* arrested.

There was a guardhouse at the front gate of the reserve, and we were herded in there. We stood, seven of us, around a bare wooden table under a bulb that was shedding a pessimistic yellow light, while Paul's brick of hashish was poked and prodded. 'What this?' demanded one of the policeman (who, we were slowly realising, may not have been a policeman after all; perhaps he was just a guard, on duty for the reserve we'd unwittingly stumbled into). 'This drugs! This drugs!'

Paul held out his hands, palms up. 'I'm an American,' he said. 'I have headaches. This is my medicine. It is medicine for headaches.'

One of the guards turned on him. 'You lie!' he hissed. 'This marijuana!'

Paul smiled the slow, knowing smile of the truly stoned. 'Don't be silly, man,' he said. 'You know what marijuana looks like. This isn't marijuana.'

The guards (there were, we now realised, only four of them, not the phalanx we'd imagined earlier; and those weren't guns they were holding, but night-sticks) huddled together and whispered. Then the top guy pulled back, turned to us, and said, 'Go.' And then he *gave the hashish brick back to Paul.*

We piled out of the guard house, hardly able to believe what had just happened. But what happened next is a million times more unbelievable: Paul leant back like a cricketer who'd caught a ball on the boundary and had only this one chance to run out a high-scoring batsman, and, making sure the betraying wind was behind him, *tossed the hashish brick down the ravine.*

It was gone. We were devastated. I said to him, 'You poes.' The others weren't South African and they didn't understand the word, but they got the meaning.

At about 2 that morning we drove back down to Pattaya in our convoy of Jeeps and motorcycles. We gathered on the beach to wait for the launch that would take us back to the ship. The adrenaline and THC had burned off and the mood was sombre.

We dragged sunbeds out from a vendor's stall and arranged them, silent and somewhat depressed, on the beach. Another vendor came past and we paid a dollar apiece for mosquito coils to keep the little critters at bay.

As I lay down on my sunbed and wriggled around a bit to get comfortable, thinking to catch a few zees before the launch came in, I felt something dig me in the hip. 'Hey,' I said to my compadres, 'guess what I've just found in my pocket?'

So, amid much cheerful back-slapping, I made a nice little joint out of the matchbox of marijuana I'd so irresponsibly retrieved on pain of dying in a Thai prison. We smoked it, sitting on the beach, and even the lavish and noisome crapping of the pair of elephants that were browsing in the undergrowth just out of sight couldn't spoil the mood.

When the launch came in in the morning, I climbed on and sat right at the front of the boat. It picked up speed in the quiet dawn air, skimming over the wavetops. With the rising sun at my back, the shimmering sea beneath me, and the hulking shadow of the *QE2* lying out at anchor, waiting to welcome us 'home', I have seldom felt so free. And so happy.

§

The same couldn't be said for Alan, one of only two black waiters on board during a stop in Japan. Recreational drugs of any description were in woefully short supply in Japan, so when Alan went on shore leave, he took with him a bag of dope he'd procured elsewhere.

When he came back from his time ashore, it was in a taxi – and for reasons not known to us but which probably had something to do with his altered mental state, he decided on an impulse not to pay the taxi driver. Instead, he flung open the door and hotfooted it up the *QE2* gangway – not realising that in his haste to exit the vehicle, he'd dropped his dope stash on the floor of the taxi.

It was a matter of very short work for the taxi driver to come on board and, given the choice between the only two black staff members, one of whom was clear-eyed and lucid (if enormously irritated at having been dragged out of bed for this impromptu identity parade), and the other wild-eyed and giggling, to identify Alan. He might have got away with a slap on the wrist for trying to stiff the taxi driver, but the dagga he'd dropped did for him, and he ended up serving six months in jail in Japan.

11. The Outside Decks

Among the favourite hangouts when the weather is good for everyone on a cruise ship, crew and passengers alike, are the outdoor decks. There's something about being out there, miles from land, with no light pollution and the stars hanging so low it looks like you can touch them, and the ocean drifting past, that pulls people into the outdoors.

Sometimes a chemical bioluminescence created by groups of single-celled plankton called dinoflagellates would make the sea glow bright green. This phenomenon, sometimes known as a 'milky sea', is a result of the planktons' defensive behaviour. It's occasionally so bright that it interferes with marine navigation; in 2005, a 15 000-square-kilometre spread of milky sea off the coast of Africa was visible from space. This magical natural event would lure passengers outside, where they'd hang over the railings, and a gentle party atmosphere would prevail.

On the world cruises, when the ship spent much time in tropical and subtropical climes, the outdoor decks were often packed with people. Not so, however, on the five-day North Atlantic crossings, for the simple reason that, in spite of it being summer, the weather was often cold and misty – it wasn't unusual for passengers to spend the entire crossing indoors, playing games, watching movies, eating in the restaurants, sitting in the pubs and going to shows.

Which made the hullaballoo we often went through on leaving Southampton for these crossings both pointless and intensely irritating. These North Atlantic crossings were characterised by advance bookings of various kinds – passengers coming on board reserved, for instance, salon appointments, seats at shows and tables in restaurants ahead of their embarkation. They also reserved deck chairs, and there lay the rub: for many passengers, the prebooking of their deck chairs was their metaphorical 'putting their towel down', and they were anxious, on getting on board, to make sure that 'their' deck chair was duly booked.

So we'd always have a dozen or so whittering little old ladies flapping around as we left Southampton, asking us repeatedly to double-check that their deck chair had their name on it, causing all manner of additional administrative labour, when we knew damned fine that it was very likely that they'd never so much as poke their noses out of their cabins for the entire crossing.

For the ship's crew, there was another reason for loving the outdoor decks: the amazing selection of dagga available on board.

On 2 Deck Aft there were fourteen bollards, used to tether the ship to the quay when it was in port. This deck wasn't open to passengers, and most sea evenings when the weather was good, each of the bollards would be topped by a backgammon board; and around each board crew members would gather to dobbel and skinner.

But the really interesting thing about these fourteen bollards was the comprehensive tour of the marijuana world they offered. The *QE2* employed people from all over the globe, so a wander from the first bollard to the last might involve a small toke from joints made of any number of different strains of marijuana: Panama Red; Acapulco Gold from Mexico; BC Bud out of Canada; Kush, the pride of Pakistan and Northern India; the USA's Northern Lights; Chocolate Thai; Malawi Gold; and, of course, South Africa's own darling, Durban Poison. I'd stalk onto 2 Deck Aft feeling strung-out and tired and peeved; and I'd drift off the other end of it, seriously chuffed to be alive.

Another favourite place for a spliff was the very top deck of the ship, where the funnel (or stack) was situated, just above what we called Doggie Deck because there were eight dog kennels up there for people who travelled with their pets (plus a lamppost for them to pee on!). Here, you could really get away from the hurdy-gurdy of the ship – sitting right under the stars, with the 21-metre funnel gently swaying from side to side (which it did even when the ship was going through still oceans) was a special treat. The funnel deck was also the girls' sunbathing deck and declared off-limits when there were women sunning themselves – a bit annoying for we men when we wanted to go up there (as if we hadn't seen a pair of tits before!).

The ship was docked in Sydney, Australia for that country's bicentennial celebrations in 1988. I'd spent the day with my friend, Brita, who lived in the city, and that evening we went back aboard and climbed up to Doggie Deck. We sat there to watch the most amazing fireworks display on the Sydney Harbour Bridge. It was an evening that both Brita and I will always remember.

§

The Pool Deck was the domain of an astoundingly energetic 'pool boy' called Lee (dubbed 'Flea' for his small size and boundless vigour). His official job was to provide towels, cushions and other poolside accoutrements for the passengers, and also to keep the pool area free of debris like used crockery and glasses. His unofficial job was to get his leg over as many times a day as possible, and he was as good at this as he was at stacking towels.

He used for his romantic assignations the towel locker on the Pool Deck, which was barely big enough to turn around in, never mind anything else. But shipboard gossip said that he sometimes had sex with up to three women in a day there, and I had no reason to disbelieve it.

§

The upper outer decks were the place I experienced two passages I'll never forget. The first was in 1986, when the *QE2* traversed the Straits of Magellan, down at the very bottom of the world, between Chile and Tierra del Fuego. The waterway is named for Portuguese explorer Ferdinand Magellan, who first navigated it in 1520. It's notorious for its difficult navigability (not least because of its narrowness in places – only two kilometres wide at its thinnest point) and its inhospitable climate, often being very foggy and stormy.

For that navigation of the Straits, however, the weather was kind, and we were treated to a magical sunset. It felt almost otherworldly to be on this massive vessel on what amounted to a river that wound through what seemed to be a series of swamps.

And I remember it most particularly because it was another record-breaker for the *QE2*: it was the first time ever a passenger cruise ship had done the journey. It's always nice to be present when history is made.

The other passage was a regular one on the world itinerary – the *QE2* had been doing it annually since 1975 – but no less fascinating for that: through the Panama Canal, a manmade waterway joining the Caribbean Sea and the Pacific Ocean. When the *QE2* passed through the canal for the first time in 1975, it was the largest passenger ship ever to do so – leaving, at its narrowest point, just inches to spare on either side as it traversed the locks – and set another record, that for paying the highest toll, $100 000. But since using the canal cut about 8 000 miles off a journey that would otherwise go all the way around South America, this was no doubt considered worth it.

(Equally famously, the lowest toll was charged to American adventurer and writer Richard Halliburton, who swam through the canal in 1928, paying 36c to do so.)

The canal is made up of a series of six massive locks, fed by two dams. Electronic towing locomotives called mules, three on either side of the ship, haul the vessel through the locks. These mules were of special interest to some of the *QE2* crew, as their operators often doubled as small-time dope pedlars, and we were able – despite the beady eye kept on all by ship security – to replenish our dagga stocks during the day-long traverse. So while the passengers gorged themselves on the ice cream feast put on by the *QE2* to while away the hours of the long, hot Panama passage, we stocked up with soft-serve of our own.

12. Disembarkation

Anyone who's travelled globally knows that red tape is part of the procedure, and with the *QE2* famously stopping in 41 cities of 25 nations on five continents in 109 days on its world tour, red tape inescapably came with the cruise.

For the ship's travellers, this process was made a little easier by some preparatory administration: the emigration officials of the next country we'd be stopping at would join the ship at its previous stop, and during the few days it took us to reach their country, would process all passports and visas, so that by the time we docked, most passengers and crew were free to wander down the gangway and go in search of new and exciting experiences.

Not so, in those days, South Africans. For many years I was the only South African crew member on board the liner, and there were several port stops during which I was confined to the ship, Kenya and India being two I remember fairly vividly – in between uselessly pacing the decks, half-mad with boredom, I had to report back to the onboard immigration officials every hour on the hour, so they could be sure I hadn't jumped ship to wreak untold South African-style havoc in their beloved countries.

Trying to get a visa for me to step onto dry land in Australia was a particularly enlightening experience. The crew purser, who was responsible for organising these things, sent my passport ahead to New York with an application in it for an Australian visa. It was turned down. So when we left New York, he had my passport and the application sent on to Los Angeles, our next port of call. It was refused there too, and the purser, not a man to let red tape entangle him, had it couriered on to Honolulu. There, I was refused an Australian visa. Japan said no too, and so did Fiji. Finally, there was only New Zealand left before we reached Australia, and, with my passport resembling a Christmas tree it had so many 'visa denied' stamps in it, I'd resigned myself to being confined to deck while my mates went ashore to meet Sheilas and Bruces and have fun with beer and barbies.

But then two Aussie immigration officials got on board in New Zealand and were refreshingly frank in their requirements: 'Give us a bottle of grog and two cartons of smokes, and we'll stamp him in,' they said. So after practically circumnavigating the world and being denied entry into Australia at just about every port of call, twenty packs of Marlboros and a bottle of whisky saw me safely into Oz. Ain't corruption fabulous?

Interestingly enough, I never had a problem getting in to Spain – until Nelson Mandela gave a speech on a visit to Cuba in 1991 that included the exhortation, 'Long live the Cuban Revolution; long live comrade Fidel Castro…' From that point until I left the *QE2*, neither love nor money could get me, a South African, onto land in that sea port. (For the record, I personally was no fan of Fidel's.)

As a South African, it was weird, too, for me to see the reverse-racism card played in these mind-boggling bureaucratic machinations. Once, en route to Barbados, the purser was going through the crew manifest with the Barbadian immigration officials, who zeroed in on my nationality. 'South African,' one of them said, poking a finger at the clipboard with unnecessary zeal. 'Not allowed.'

The purser looked amused. 'Why not?' he said.

'South Africans aren't permitted,' said the official, irritably.

'But he's as black as the ace of spades,' said the purser.

There were immediate huge yawning smiles all round. 'Then of course he can go ashore!' the official said, generously.

The purser came to me as I was about to go down the gangway. 'Behave yourself, Japie,' he warned. 'Remember, you're an honorary black man.'

One memorable disembarkation for me was my first 'home' one – fourteen months after I'd begun cruising, I got my first official leave and was due to get off the ship in Cape Town. The night before we pulled into the dock the crew held a huge party for me – they really pulled out all the stops and it was 6am before I stumbled, sloshing with alcohol, into my bunk.

I had, of course, let my mother know that I was on my way home and she couldn't wait to see me. In fact, so keen was she to make sure I got a proper welcome home that she got together a deputation of friends and family to meet me at the harbour. They arrived in several car loads, carrying balloons, streamers and banners reading 'Welcome home, Richard!'

I didn't know this – and so hard had I partied the night before that I am ashamed to admit that when the ship cruised into the harbour, I was still sawing logs down in my cabin. My welcoming party eagerly searched the rails for my face but without success. The ship docked, the gangway was lowered, and people began streaming off. I was not among them.

Now, in the letters I'd written home during the year or so I'd been away, I'd made no secret about the long, arduous hours the salon kept. It's probably fair to say that I'd made a fairly big deal of it, in fact. So when the stream of people disembarking finally became a trickle, and I still hadn't made my appearance, my mother turned in disgust to the gathered welcoming party and sniffed, 'I bet they made him work!'

(There was other staff who worked as long and hard. The cruise director, whose office was in charge of all onboard entertainment and daily programmes, was one such. Sometimes he was so tired by the time he dropped into my chair for his monthly trim that I'd have to enlist the help of another stylist – to hold his head up while I cut his hair, as he would fall straight to sleep the minute he relaxed.)

§

When the ship could go all the way into port, as in Cape Town, disembarking passengers wasn't a problem. There were several ports that were too small to accommodate the *QE2*, however, and here we were required to ferry passengers from the liner, moored outside the port, into harbour.

Where suitable tenders weren't available, we would use the *QE2*'s launches to transport the passengers. But there were places where the tenders weren't particularly suitable and yet we were forced to use them nonetheless, and this was usually linked to some form of corruption. In India, for instance, the palms of practically every minister of every department in local government had to be greased before passengers were allowed to disembark – and then the ship was also required to hire, at hefty expense, the Indian port authority's ferries to take the passengers in. These launches were never in good repair, and it was a delicate matter to explain to passengers who'd paid gigantic sums of money for the honour of cruising on the *QE2* why they should have to ride these squalid boats in to shore.

One disembarkation I remember in particular was in Thailand, another port that insisted on using its own ferries – although 'ferries' here is a loose term, because what they sent out were a series of dug-out canoes. It required teeth-aching tact to balance out the variously shaped and weighted septuagenarians, one on this side and the other on that, to ensure the dugout wouldn't capsize during the ride into harbour.

Another was in Monte Carlo, where the weather was so foul that the fifteen-minute launch-ride back to the ship turned into a makeshift horror movie, with passengers succumbing to seasickness and, in one case, falling over and injuring himself so badly that the ferry floor was awash with blood. I'd done many ferry-trips to and from the ship by that time, but I must admit even I was a bit frightened: once or twice, with our little launch stuck between waves so tall they looked like office blocks, I seriously doubted we'd make it back to the *QE2*.

Ours was the last launch in that night: Cunard put up everyone else who was still ashore – including staff, blast them! – in five-star hotels, and sent the launches in to fetch them late the next morning, when the weather had settled.

An embarkation I remember vividly was in 1992, in Lima, Peru, when the president of that country, Alberto Fujimori, went on national television to announce an *autogolpe* (or 'self-coup'). With military backing, he dissolved Congress, suspended civil liberties and established government by decree. Tanks rolled in to Lima and soldiers began arresting lawmakers, journalists and opposition politicians.

The *QE2* staff sprang into action to round up our passengers, hurrying them onto the ship in preparation for an earlier-than-scheduled departure from the embattled city. We were very proud of ourselves as we ticked off the last passenger and the ship began moving away from the port, which by then was resounding with gunfire.

Alas, in his haste the captain had forgotten about a sandbank in the middle of the harbour, and we ran aground.

There followed a tense few hours while we all crouched on board, listening to the havoc back on land, waiting for the tide to rise high enough to float us off.

§

The occasional forced disembarkation of passengers did happen too. One passenger lost his head on board and was disembarked in Barbados, deemed a danger to himself and an embarrassment to the other passengers. Poor old fellow, who knows what short-circuited in his brain, but the first I knew of him was when he wandered, stark naked, into the salon reception and enquired of me, somewhat querulously, 'And what time is it, young man?'

You may think I should have found his unclothed state alarming, but we were trained not to let anything passengers did ruffle us. So I turned to the large clock mounted on the wall behind me, clearly visible to the bare-arsed chap, and said, pointedly, 'Ten to one.'

'Thank you,' he said, and turned and shuffled out, his little bum winking pinkly in the salon's lights.

Two minutes later he was back, every bit as naked as the first time. 'And what time is it, young man?' he asked me.

Oh boy. I turned to the wall clock and said, even more pointedly, 'Eight minutes to one.'

'Thank you,' he said, and meandered away.

My last view of the watchless wonder passenger was on the pier in Barbados. Still utterly unclothed, he was being restrained by men in white coats as the ship sailed away from the harbour. He stared up in desperate incomprehension then, as I watched, he broke free of his captors and ran screaming down the pier. 'Wait! Wait! Come back! Come back!' he shouted. I could still hear the frantic tone of his voice when I went to sleep that night.

We also had, somewhat excitingly, a man overboard. This was on a crossing from Southampton to New York and during the captainship of Lawrence Portet, described by journalist Bryan Appleyard in the UK's *The Times* in May 1987 as 'an immensely tall Bernie Winters lookalike' who 'beams at one and all and absorbs complaints with an eerie air of unconcern' and whose sense of humour seemed 'a touch awry'.

Appleyard got it right on the button. When the very anxious wife of the missing man reported her husband's disappearance to the purser, the normal routine was followed, as per captain's orders: after a fast, thorough search of all conceivable nooks and crannies of the ship by every hand available, the time and place of the unfortunate man's last known whereabouts was established, and the ship turned around. Reaching the spot the man had last been seen, the two crash boats at the front of the ship were dropped – crash boats are fast, efficient vessels that can be put into the water immediately and are built to handle rough conditions.

A thorough search of the sea by boat and spotlight (and, by that time, by practically all the passengers, who were cramming the decks for a possible sighting) failed to locate the missing man, and Captain Portet made the decision to continue with the cruise. 'Ladies and gentlemen, we've done a thorough reconnaissance of the area and we haven't located the missing passenger,' he said (or words to this effect) in his deep, booming voice over the tannoy system. 'Frankly, if he went over the front of the ship, the barnacles on the ship's bottom would have done for him or he'd have been caught in the propellers. And if they didn't, the freezing cold temperature of the sea would have. So we're resuming our voyage.'

Who knows how the traumatised wife/widow took this. We salon staff went up on deck later and threw a few roses into the sea to say goodbye to the castaway, so lamentably unlamented by the captain.

We had two other disappearances on board during the time I was cruising. One was a married couple who both signed on in New York but the husband of which had gone missing by the time we reached the mid-Atlantic. We followed procedure (search the ship, turn back, search the sea) but the man couldn't be found. When we docked in Southampton the Fraud Squad was waiting for the wife, and they took great pleasure in frog-marching her down the gangway. The husband, it turned out, was wanted for some massive insurance heist, and had snuck ashore before the ship left New York, leaving his wife to declare him lost at sea.

The other one was heart-wrenching. It was a single man who'd come on board unaccompanied in New York and who was discovered to be missing many hours, and maybe even days, after the ship had left harbour. Because nobody could pinpoint when he'd last been seen, no effort was ever made to find him. What I found particularly touching was how he'd left his cabin: immaculate in all respects, except for his life vest, which he'd carefully laid out on his bed. It seemed to me a profound cry for help, and the image of it stayed with me for a very long time.

(Interestingly, a report by the cruise industry in 2008 said that more than thirty passengers had disappeared from ships in the five preceding years, and that this didn't include those who were known to be suicides or drunken accidents. One of these was a 62-year-old German woman, Sabine L, who was a passenger, along with her husband and two friends, on the *QE2* in 2006. Last seen when the ship was somewhere off Madeira, Sabine L was never found.)

§

One of my own disembarkations was particularly meaningful for me. It was in Namibia's Walvis Bay, a natural deep-water harbour on the Kuiseb River delta on southern Africa's west coast – the only harbour of any size along that coast, in fact. Walvis Bay is situated between the Atlantic Ocean and the 'dune sea' of the Namib Desert, which stretches for about 1 600 kilometres along the coast of Namibia. This desert, one of the oldest in the world, gets only about 10 mm of rain annually and is almost completely barren. It's famous for its monumental sand dunes which, at Sossusvlei, reach up to 300 metres high.

Ten years previously, at the tender age of 18, I'd been doing my mandatory national service for the then-South African Defence Force and, as a result of some infringement, had been sent to 2 SAI (Second South African Infantry) in the town of Walvis Bay. The 2 SAI base was notoriously bleak: there were no camp walls because even if you did decide to go AWOL, where were you going to go, with the sea on one side and nothing but miles and miles of desert between you and anything resembling civilisation on the other?

The stilted buildings had been erected after the Second World War as temporary military accommodation and were still being used for this purpose, without any visible upgrade or refurbishment, forty years later.

The climatic conditions were equally miserable: none of the windows in the bungalows could open, as the hinges had all rusted off, and it was very difficult to keep anything clean up to inspection level: everything was coated in a fine layer of salt within a few hours – rifles had to be cleaned and oiled twice a day to prevent rusting. The camp also had a unique 'water parade' every morning: troepies were expected to drink about two litres of water before the day's activities began, to prevent dehydration in the mercilessly dry, salt-laden desert air.

It was to this hellish place that I was sent, not many months after I'd left school, on a five-day train trip from Port Elizabeth. Walvis Bay is the terminus of the trans-Namib railway to the country's capital, Windhoek; the final night's journey is between Windhoek and Walvis Bay.

I clearly recall waking up on that final morning, with the train moving so slowly that it was possible to get out and walk alongside it. After five days cooped up inside, that's exactly what I and several other young soldiers did: the image of that slow-moving train, the desolate and neverending surrounding desert, and the rank smell of old fish blowing from the bay on a hot wind, has never left me. I was to be in Walvis Bay for six months, and I thought my life had ended.

The experience was every bit as ghastly as I'd expected, but one good thing did come out of it: it was at 2 SAI that I met a Capetonian called Russel, who later persuaded me to move from Port Elizabeth to Cape Town and thus put in motion the chain of events that would eventually see me end up as chief hairdresser on the *QE2*.

And it was as chief hairdresser, ten years later, that I next saw Walvis Bay. As it happened, the liner was approaching the harbour early in the morning, and there in the distance, pushing into the town at walking pace, was the trans-Namib train.

Knowing that we'd be stopping in Walvis, I'd told some of my favourite clients that I'd spent six months there doing national service. They were disbelieving, and when one of them asked if I'd take her to the camp, I thought, why not? She was joined by some of her friends and, once the ship had moored, I quickly arranged for a luxury bus to come and fetch us.

Conscription wasn't abolished in South Africa until 1994 (the same year that Walvis Bay was finally transferred from South African sovereignty to the newly independent Namibia), so we were able to surprise some troepies on parade. I'll never forget the wide-eyed look of astonishment on the face of the youngster raising the flag as six fur-coated, jewel-bedecked, perfectly coiffed and manicured American ladies and I rolled into 2 SAI.

Heading back to the ship after our visit, in airconditioned opulence, accompanied by a small group of some of the world's most indulged people, and knowing that when I got back on board, it would be to champagne cocktails, before once again setting off across the world's oceans in one of the most famous luxury cruise liners ever to have sailed, I thought, 'You've come a long way, baby!'

A potted history of the QE2

The *RMS Queen Elizabeth 2* (the 'QE2') was owned and operated by Cunard Lines from 1967 to 2008, when it was decommissioned and sold for $100 million. It has since been permanently moored in Dubai.

Built at a cost of £29 million, it was launched in September 1967 by Queen Elizabeth II, using the same pair of gold scissors her mother and grandmother had used to launch the *Queen Elizabeth* and *Queen Mary*, respectively. The *QE2* completed its maiden voyage from Southampton to New York in May 1969.

Sailing out of Southampton, England, the *QE2* was 294 metres in length, 52 metres high and had a beam of 32 metres; it carried up to 1 800 passengers and 1 050 officers and crew. Before being refitted with a diesel power plant in 1986, it was the last oil-fired steam-turbine passenger steamship crossing the Atlantic in scheduled liner service.

The year it came into service, 1969, was also the year of the *Apollo II* space mission and the unveiling of the Concorde. In keeping with these racy times, Cunard broke from the traditional interiors of their previous liners, and used modern materials like plastic laminates, aluminium and Plexiglas. Furniture was modular, and abstract art decorated the public rooms and cabins. (This was changed in later refurbishments.)

The *QE2* saw some excitement during its reign of the world's oceans. In 1971 it participated in the rescue of some 500 passengers from the burning French ship the *Antilles*, which had run aground near Mustique. The *Antilles* capsized and sank the next day and the passengers were landed in Barbados.

In 1979 the ship had to change course to avoid a hurricane which covered 1 380 miles of the North Atlantic with waves of sixty feet high. No cooking on stoves was allowed and passengers had to live on sandwiches and salads. The ship docked in New York three days behind schedule.

In 1982 the *QE2* was refitted for service in the Falklands War, with the installation of three helicopter pads over the swimming pools, the transformation of public lounges into dormitories, and the covering of carpets with 2 000 sheets of hardboard. The ship carried 3 000 troops and 650 volunteer crew to the south Atlantic.

In 1986 the *QE2* underwent a huge overhaul that changed its propulsion system from steam to diesel-electric. It also received the first-ever TV transmissions at sea, including *NBC Nightly News* and the US Superbowl. The same year the first baby was born on board.

In August 1992, the ship's hull was extensively damaged when it ran aground near Martha's Vineyard in the USA. The passengers were evacuated and the ship taken out of service while repairs were made.

In 1994 the *QE2* was given a multimillion-dollar refurbishment. Almost all of the remaining original decor was replaced, with Cunard opting to return to the line's traditional style. Five years later the ship was treated to yet another multi-million-dollar refurbishment.

In 1996 the first satellite transmission of a TV programme from a ship at sea went out from the *QE2* and the first seagoing branch of Harrods opened aboard. In the same year, during its twentieth world cruise, the ship passed its four-millionth-mile mark – the *QE2* had sailed the equivalent of 185 times around the planet.

In 1998, as part of his 80th birthday celebrations, President Nelson Mandela and his wife Graca Machel sailed from Durban to Cape Town on the *QE2*.

The *QE2* left Southampton for the last time on 11 November 2008, seen off by a huge fireworks display, a flotilla of smaller craft and thousands of well-wishers. By this time, the ship had sailed over six million nautical miles (equivalent to travelling to the moon and back 13 times), been around the world 25 times, carried 2,5 million passengers and completed 806 trans-Atlantic crossings.

In 2013, plans were announced to convert the *QE2* into a floating luxury hotel. The 990 staterooms will be converted into 400 luxury suites, the ballroom will be refurbished, and there will be seven restaurants, ten lounges, a cinema, a museum with *QE2* memorabilia, and a mall. The work is due to be completed by 2015.

§

Today, on any given week, Steiner employees at sea massage over 30 000 bodies, deep-cleanse 15 000 faces, blowdry 6 000 heads of hair, and manicure about 6 000 pairs of hands.

Glossary of South African terms

babbelas – bad hangover

bliksem – hit or punch

dagga – marijuana

dobbel – gamble

Japie – derogatory term for a South African; from 'plaasjapie', or 'farm boy'

jol, jolling – a party; having a good time

klap – slap (Afrikaans); or quickly finished (as in 'we klapped a jug of sangria')

loopdop – last drink; 'one for the road' (Afrikaans)

moffie – homosexual

piraat – very proper (Afrikaans)

poephol – arsehole

poes – swear-word; Afrikaans equivalent of 'cunt'

Prestik – South African equivalent of Blu-tak

skeef – suspiciously sideways (as in 'skeef look')

skinner – gossip (Afrikaans); more properly, 'skinder'

snotklap – literally, 'snot smack' (Afrikaans), meaning to hit so hard you cause snot to fly

Spur – popular value-for-money family steakhouse-type eatery

stop – (of dagga): smallish quantity of dagga, usually wrapped in newspaper

troepie – South African Defence Force foot soldier

About the authors

During his cruising career, qualified hairdresser **Richard Wood** worked on over 100 ocean-going vessels in various capacities, although his main commitment was as Steiner's chief hairdresser on the *QE2*. He was born in Port Elizabeth and educated in Grahamstown. He now lives and works – as a hairdresser – in a small Western Cape town.

Tracey Hawthorne has published award-winning corporate e-newsletters, produced four natural-history guides, co-authored a book on South African schools, written a biography of swimming sensation Natalie du Toit and another of world-renowned artist John Meyer, and contributed to several other works, including travel guides, the *Platter* wine guides, and an anthology of short stories by South African women.

Printed in Great Britain
by Amazon.co.uk, Ltd.,
Marston Gate.